MIND-BENDING MATH AND SCIENCE ACTIVITIES FOR GIFTED STUDENTS (GRADES K–12)

Rosemary Callard-Szulgit
Greg Karl Szulgit

Rowman & Littlefield Education
Lanham, Maryland • Toronto • Oxford
2006

Published in the United States of America
by Rowman & Littlefield Education
A Division of Rowman & Littlefield Publishers, Inc.
A wholly owned subsidiary of The Rowman & Littlefield Publishing Group, Inc.
4501 Forbes Boulevard, Suite 200, Lanham, Maryland 20706
www.rowmaneducation.com

PO Box 317
Oxford
OX2 9RU, UK

British Library Cataloguing in Publication Information Available

Library of Congress Cataloging-in-Publication Data

Callard-Szulgit, Rosemary, 1946-
  Mind-bending math and science activities for gifted students (grades K–12) /
Rosemary S. Callard-Szulgit, Greg Karl Szulgit.
    p. cm.
  Includes bibliographical references.
  ISBN 1-57886-317-1 (pbk. : alk. paper)
  1. Mathematics—Study and teaching (Middle schools)—Activity programs.
2. Science—Study and teaching (Middle schools)—Activity programs. 3.
Gifted children—Education. I. Szulgit, Greg Karl, 1968- II. Title.
QA16.C35 2006
372.7—dc22

                                                                    2005019292

∞™ The paper used in this publication meets the minimum requirements of
American National Standard for Information Sciences—Permanence of
Paper for Printed Library Materials, ANSI/NISO Z39.48-1992.
Manufactured in the United States of America.

I have such a special love and admiration for my husband, Karl—a brilliant man, exceptional educator, devoted father, friend, colleague, and credit union leader. Your love and brilliance for math earned you the respect and admiration of all members in WIT Federal Credit Union, as well as throughout the state and nation. I still remember the day you won the longest drive contest for men at a CU Golf Tournament and they announced you as "grandfather" of the credit unions in New York State rather than the "father," as you were so fondly known. You will always be known as their father—forever young! Karl, always my beloved (August 12, 1931–October 5, 2004).

With special love to our children, Fern, Eric, Greg, and Mark, and our adored grandson, Olin.

Special regards to Lyn Reville, whose friendship I have appreciated since we met at SUNY Potsdam in 1964. It appears we will be growing old together, helping each other out and laughing along the way.

Sincere thanks also to Laura, Ann, Heather, Diane, Jeanette, and Shelly for your complete support, help, and love given me after Karl's passing. You continue to fill my heart with genuine love.

CONTENTS

PART THREE: TECHNOLOGY/BUSINESS OPPORTUNITIES

PART FOUR: STILL MORE ACTIVITIES

PART FIVE: ACADEMIC ENVIRONS

PART SIX: REFLECTIONS ON EDUCATION

Appendices

PREFACE

What does it take for a student to be brilliant? Certainly it entails a healthy dose of intelligence, but I think there also has to be an aspect of illumination mixed with it. A student needs to take his or her "book smarts" and electrify that trait with creativity and imagination. Memorizing the Periodic Table of chemical elements is a neat parlor trick that requires quite a bit of brain power, but it's the brilliant student who will think of a new way to organize the elements in that table. Playing a piece of music flawlessly requires talent and discipline, but the performance will not be brilliant until the student makes the music speak in a new voice via his or her own interpretation. Intelligence is impressive, but brilliance is inspiring.

The material in this book is not meant to replace existing curricula—nor is it a panacea for bored or underachieving students. Instead, the literary suggestions, exercises, competitions, and so forth are meant to help students unlock creative potentials and combine them with intellectual rigor. Parents, teachers, and students should use this book as a guide toward finding opportunities that they may not have known about previously, allowing them to "take off" in whatever direction inspires them the most. Each student in question will "click" with different chapters, and if each is significantly inspired by just one idea within, then we will rest easily knowing that we have made a positive contribution to education.

We have included a few exercises that we have written in a student-friendly fashion. They can be copied and given to students, who should be able to follow the instructions with minimal guidance. In that sense, the assignments will grant teachers more freedom with their time, because they can meet with the students at convenient checkpoints. This does not, however, abdicate teachers from their responsibility to spend time with those students. As bright as they may be, they still benefit from a teacher's guidance in helping them reach higher levels of thinking. Keep in touch with them and let them inspire you.

INTRODUCTION

While growing up, I knew my mother was a brilliant woman. I also knew my dad was exceedingly smart. In my adult years, I have been blessed with a brilliant husband, Karl, whose genius intellect and enormous love for learning, while encompassing the grandeur of life, has brought me a far greater understanding of the unparalleled joys of thinking and the freedom to learn without limits!

As a child, I loved working with the other young children every week in Sunday school. I have always loved spinning magic with students in my own classrooms. Once I graduated from college and became an "official" teacher, I continued to be exhilarated, sharing the excitement of learning. Now, as my graduate students and I meet weekly, we leave classes pretty much "pumped up," even if we're all a wee bit tired at 9:30 p.m. There is such a joy in learning for every one of us when we take our knowledge and understanding to the synthesis level. Glorious understanding and phenomenal creativity abound in synthesis! Yet, for hundreds of thousands of our children, the education process is fraught with endless hours of homework every night, riddled with continual stresses and anxiety over constant tests, grading, and continual evaluations. We all know scores of children who were avid readers as youngsters, devouring book after book, engulfed in the pleasure and interest of reading, only to stop reading for pleasure by fourth or fifth grade once the multitude of "assigned" readings and books became a part of nightly homework assignments. Add book reports, novel dissections, vocabulary lists, word definitions, and sentence development, and reading for joy became lost in the dark forests of homework requirements.

By the third grade, gifted girls and boys have already developed the habits and expectations of receiving an A grade on their work and report cards, primarily because they already know the grade-level work being taught and tested. Girls are already claiming math is hard, while boys are beginning to opt out of reading and language arts activities.

One result of the U.S. Department of Education's Individuals with Disabilities Education Act (Public Law 105–17) is the placement of additional numbers of special-education students in our already crowded, heterogeneously grouped classrooms. Special education teachers work as consultants in conjunction with classroom teachers, where students with disabilities are served completely within the general education classroom.

This helps provide wonderful additional support and services for our identified special-education students. However, we continue to fall short on honoring and providing support services, training, and personnel for our identified gifted students.

In November 2004, a special panel was created in New York State's Education Department to examine math standards and to propose sweeping changes in what math topics are taught and when they are tested, particularly at the middle and secondary levels. One of the thirteen recommendations included starting some math subjects earlier, including algebra in grade 5. Why not bring algebra and other subjects to first and second graders who are capable of learning at a pace and level well beyond that of their grade-level peers?

Gifted children are, by definition (Ross 1993, 26),

Children and youth with outstanding talent who perform or show the potential for performing at remarkably high levels of accomplishment when compared with others of their age, experience or environment.

These children and youth exhibit high-performance capability in intellectual, creative and/or artistic areas, possess an unusual leadership capacity, or excel in specific academic fields. They require services or activities not ordinarily provided by the school.

With this book, we hope to provide an easier access to specialized information for teachers, parents, and students whose interests, drive, and creative thinking will forge new paths in the areas of science and mathematics. In the understanding that what works for gifted children works for all children, we give you this book. May it be one more beacon of light in the quest for understanding and helping our gifted children and their teachers.

With sincerity,
Rosemary

If a teacher or parent were to ask me what the best program, activity, or outlet is to foster a student's intelligence, I would have to say that it doesn't much matter, as long as the student becomes engaged in his or her own learning. Choice and creative freedom are important catalysts that can decide the difference between a chore and a fulfilling experience. This is not to suggest that learning should always be "exciting and fun"; far from it. Hard work and discipline are a valuable part of the process, and students *want* to be challenged. It is my experience that allowing students to have a hand in directing their own learning increases their retention, integration, and synthesis-level thinking, which are often the basic education goals that we are trying to achieve.

A second point of great importance is for the student to interact with others who "get" them; those of a similar ilk. I vividly remember joining the Academic Decathlon team in high school, as it was a new culture to me. I was not used to being with people who would take a Saturday morning to study as a team. Something clicked in me when I realized that these people, whom I had previously thought were geeks, were really cool! Once that notion took hold, I began to be influenced by the team culture. For example, I wanted to get better grades, which was a big step forward for me, as I had always worn my "underachieving" status as a badge of honor because I had associated it with different, creative, and deeper thinking that didn't focus on mundane school tasks. My success, after much hard work, in Academic Decathlon helped me to develop a concept of myself as an academic achiever who would be accepted by others whom, it turned out, I respected. This paradigm shift did more to further my academic career than I can say.

Greg K. Szulgit

RECALLED FOR REVISION

William C. Miller

August 1, 1971

Edsel Memorial High School
Anywhere, U.S.A.

Dear Parents of Our Graduates:

As you are aware, one of your offspring was graduated from our high school this June. Since that time, it has been brought to our attention that certain insufficiencies are present in our graduates, so we are recalling all students for further education.

We have learned that in the process of the instruction we provided we forgot to install one or more of the following:

- at least one salable skill;
- a comprehensive and utilitarian set of values;
- a readiness for and understanding of the responsibilities of citizenship.

A recent consumer study consisting of follow-up of our graduates has revealed that many of them have been released with defective parts. Racism and materialism are serious flaws and we have discovered they are a part of the makeup of almost all our products. These defects have been determined to be of such magnitude that the model produced in

June is considered highly dangerous and should be removed from circulation as a hazard to the nation.

Some of the equipment which was in the past classified as optional has been reclassified as standard and should be a part of every product of our school. Therefore, we plan to equip each graduate with:

- a desire to continue to learn
- a dedication to solving problems of local, national, and international concern
- several productive ways to use leisure time
- a commitment to the democratic way of life
- extensive contact with the world outside the school
- experience in making decisions

In addition, we found we had inadvertently removed from your child his interest, enthusiasm, motivation, trust, and joy. We are sorry to report that these items have been mislaid and have not been turned in at the school Lost and Found Department. If you will inform us as to the value you place on these qualities, we will reimburse you promptly by check or cash.

As you can see, it is to your interest, and vitally necessary for your safety and the welfare of all, that graduates be returned so that these errors and oversights can be corrected. We admit that it would have been more effective and less costly in time and money to have produced the product correctly in the first place, but we hope you will forgive our error and continue to respect and support your public schools.

Sincerely,

P. Dantic, Principal

I

MATH ACTIVITIES

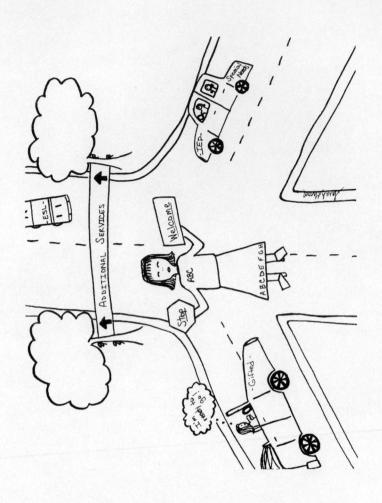

❶

CREATIVE CONVERSIONS (AND THE "SMOOT")

Greg Szulgit

Centimeters to inches, pounds to kilograms, and Celsius to Fahrenheit; we are required to do these simple conversions on a regular basis. This exercise gives students practice in measuring and converting units while also prompting them to have some fun in the process.

1. For practice, find an object on your desk and measure its length in centimeters. Now convert those units into inches. To do this, you should know that there are 2.54 centimeters in one inch. When you do the math, it is always helpful to write the units as well as the measure; that way you can "cancel out" the units and you will not get the numerator (the top number) and denominator (the bottom number) confused.

Example: If a pencil is 17.2 cm long, in inches it is:

$$17.2 \text{ cm} \times \frac{1 \text{ in}}{2.54 \text{ cm}} = \frac{6.77 \text{ in} \times \text{cm}}{\text{cm}} = 6.77 \text{ in} \times \frac{\text{cm}}{\text{cm}} = 6.77 \text{ in}$$

the units cancel

2. (a) The Harvard Bridge between Boston and Cambridge, Massachusetts, is 364.4 Smoots long. What on earth does that mean? It means that Oliver R. Smoot (a student at Massachusetts Institute of Technology in 1962) was laid down 364.4 times, end-to-end along the bridge to determine how long it was. (You might be able to find the story at http://

bmrc.berkeley.edu/people/smoot/364.4.html, or you can type "Smoots" into your favorite search engine.) Smoot was measured to be 5 feet, 7 inches tall, so approximately how long is the Harvard Bridge?

(b) Now use your own body as a unit of measure. You can call it a "me." How many me's would stretch between your school and your house? Figure out your height, the distance from your school to your house, and then do some math (a mile is 5,280 feet; a kilometer is simply 1,000 meters).

3. Invent your own units! They can be measures of time, distance, weight, volume, temperature, and so on. Try using these units to measure other common things. For example, if your pet cat (named Jasper) weighs 6 pounds, then you could figure out how many "Jaspers" you weigh. Or, if it takes you 3.5 seconds to tie your shoe, figure out how long (in "shoe tyings") your favorite TV show is.

4. Now for the next level: try combing units. For example, speed limits are posted in miles per hour (or kilometers per hour). This term has units of both distance and time. Use the examples that you invented to convert the speed limit on a local road into your units. (In the examples that I gave, I could use "me's per shoe tying," which I will abbreviate as "mes/st." Because I am 5 ft. 11 in. and can tie my shoe in 4 seconds, 60 miles/hour is equal to just about 59.5 mes/st). In other words, a car traveling 60 mph would also be traveling 59.5 of my body lengths in the time that it takes me to tie my shoe. Check your work by asking, "Does that make sense?"

2

USING MICROSOFT EXCEL AS A TEACHING TOOL

Bridgette Yaxley

This lesson utilized the program Microsoft Excel and students were asked to create their own corporation, to list their supplies, the individual cost of each supply, and how much of these supplies they would need to operate their business, using formulas to calculate what they would need to spend to begin functioning as a business. Students created the most fascinating corporations! They called them very interesting names and charted twelve months' of profit, then used the features of Excel to design a pie chart or a bar graph to show which months were most profitable overall. Some students created their own lawn mowing corporation, skateboarding shop, and a visiting nanny service. It was quite a "real world" experience for seventh graders to understand how such a computer program is truly used by actual corporations every day, and how important supply and demand really is at the end of the month and year.

Lunchtime at a *"Fast"* Food Restaurant
With a Gifted Child

3

FIGURE THIS

Rosemary Callard-Szulgit

Endorsed by the National Council of Teachers of Mathematics (NCTM), the U.S. Department of Education, and the National Science Foundation, the Figure This website (available at www.figurethis.org/index40.htm) provides oodles of math challenges for your children. The site also has a teacher's corner and a family corner, each of which includes a page on math homework tips.

What a neat way to have your students utilize computer time and have family fun together! You might want to keep a running record of math problems solved as a positive challenge and incentive to visit the site . . . one more way to enhance and enrich math studies!

4

LUNCH BUNCH

Rosemary Callard-Szulgit

To encourage extended math skills in one of the elementary buildings I was in charge of as K–8 coordinator for gifted children in the Webster Central School District, I asked the fourth-, fifth-, and sixth-grade teachers if they had a group of mathematically gifted children who might want to meet with me once a week to work on challenging math questions. The fourth-grade teachers were thrilled with my offer and opened up the opportunity to any students who might be interested.

We wound up with eight children and met from 12:05–12:35 p.m. every Thursday. I pulled the math questions from the current *Math Olympiad* book, placing on the blackboard two one-minute questions and one four-minute question to start. Students could work together or individually, however they felt most comfortable. The level of discussions and analytical thinking that went on each Thursday during lunch period made my heart beat faster with joy.

This was such a nice time together and a wonderful way to teach math skills and problem solving to interested students who already were functioning well above grade level.

In another school, our Lunch Bunch contained ten fourth, fifth, and sixth graders who were reading well beyond their grade-level peers. Again, the opportunity was extended to all and discussions of literature flourished on a weekly basis.

As an educator, I've always believed that with the greatest "affect" we obtain the greatest cognitive response from our students—all students. Lunch Bunch achieved both!

5

THE MAP PROBLEM

Greg Szulgit

Take a look at a map of the United States or any other part of the world. It seems that all of the states, provinces, or countries can be drawn in four colors without ever having any borders of the same color next to each other. Can this be right?

1. Try to draw a map that requires five colors.
   After you have given it your best shot, you might want to look here for the answer: www.math.utah.edu/~alfeld/math/4color.html
   Or try searching the web for "map problem four colors"

2. But what if the map were three-dimensional? Now how many colors would you need for any map?

6

MATH QUESTION OF THE DAY

Rosemary Callard-Szulgit

I loved doing a Math Question of the Day ("MQ of D") with my students, regardless of the grade level and age I taught. It was a great way to expose the children to approximately 120 extra math learning problems each year, aside from the specific curriculum we were working on.

The students kept a separate MQ of D notebook just for this purpose. Every morning I placed a new math question on the front board, which the students were required to write in their notebooks. They could solve them alone, with a partner, or in groups. The only requirement was the math problem needed to be solved by lunch time. The children could bring their notebooks up for the Callard-Szulgit Star of Excellence whenever they finished. Parents were also encouraged to review the math concept we covered that day and provide additional examples for their children at home.

If the math concept was completely new for the students, such as an algebra, geometry, or trigonometry problem, I would teach the concept early in the morning and do one or two math problems with the entire class.

I took the questions from Conrad and Flegler's "Math Contests," volumes 1, 2, and 3 at the elementary, middle, and high school levels.

Here's an example for you:

A *prime* number is a number greater that 1 whose only whole number factors are itself and 1. What is the smallest *prime* number greater than 50?

a) 51   b) 52   c) 53   d) 59

I also encouraged my students and parents to buy and study the types of question in these books.

I was never surprised when my students achieved the highest math scores in the school. One more great way to help kids learn, enjoy, and achieve.

7

MIND-BENDERS

Rosemary Callard-Szulgit

Most of the intellectually gifted children I've worked with loved to solve puzzles, mind-benders, or any other questions that required a challenge and/or a different style of thinking. The few children who weren't interested were usually perfectionists and fearful of making a mistake. They didn't want to deviate from their very safe routines. Making a mistake or not finding the right answers was unacceptable to them. The gifted perfectionist child is another entire topic, however, and can be studied in my book, *Perfectionism and Gifted Children* (2003b).

Allen, Gale, and Skitl (1994, 6) state that most people are content to go through life with their brain ticking over a mere fraction of its true capacity. The intention of *Mighty Mindbenders* is to present a mind workout that will "bend, stretch, and squeeze your mental powers to the very limit." This book is filled with over 200 pages of mind-boggling puzzles, brain-teasers, and mazes.

I encourage you to expose your students and own children to the variety of thinking skills and problem-solving puzzles in *Mighty Mindbenders*. Doing these activities together and in a nonthreatening intellectual environment can only excite and enhance, bend, stretch, and squeeze our children's mental powers in a stronger direction.

PLACE-VALUE GAMES

Jennifer Warren

"Place value" is a difficult math concept for some students to grasp as well as demonstrate their understanding of. The games are designed to help students demonstrate their knowledge while working at their own instructional level. The games are differentiated so that each student can work to his or her own level of ability and understanding.

HIGH ROLLIN' BOWLIN'!

In High Rollin' Bowlin'!, students bowl to knock down as many pins as desired to make the biggest number possible. If they are working on reading two-digit numbers, they will have only two pins set up and try to knock down only those pins. If they are working on reading and understanding three- or four-digit numbers, they will try to hit that many pins down and order them to make the largest number possible. If students want an extra challenge to demonstrate a full understanding of place value, they can set up all ten pins and order as many as they can knock down to make the biggest number possible. The students in all situations must be able to read the number they made.

DUCK HUNT!

In Duck Hunt!, students select a series of ducks from the pond, read the numbers on the bottom, and arrange the ducks to make the largest possible number. If they are working on two-digit numbers, the students will select only two ducks to order. If they are working on reading four-digit numbers, pupils will select four ducks to order. If they are working on six-digit numbers, they will select six ducks from the pond.

BEAN-BAG HOP!

In Bean-Bag Hop!, students use a modified twister mat and toss bean bags onto the prenumbered circles. They then try to order the numbers they landed on to make the biggest number they can. Again, this is differentiated based on student ability. If students need work on reading two digits, they toss onto only two circles. If they are working on seven digits, they will toss the bean bag seven times.

YOU SHOOT, YOU SCORE!

In You Shoot, You Score!, students use a hockey stick and puck to shoot for numbers. There is a scoring area for the students to aim at. In this area, there are the numbers from zero to nine. If they are working on reading and understanding two-digit numbers, they will shoot only twice. If they are working on higher numbers, they will shoot accordingly. The students need to record their scores and then put the numbers in order to make the biggest number they can, and then read the number aloud.

9

STOCK MARKET GAME

Rosemary Callard-Szulgit

I have loved the Stock Market Game for years. Teams of three to five students compete against each other in sessions of ten weeks, investing a hypothetical $100,000 in stocks listed on the American and New York Stock Exchanges and the NASDAQ National Market. This game is a wonderful tool for teachers to integrate lessons in finance and economics in an exciting and motivational way for their students, and is very interdisciplinary. Student transactions are computed weekly and teams receive weekly financial statements.

The Stock Market Game is available for grades 4–12 and is a national competition. Financial awards are given to the best performing teams in a geographical area.

Many times you can gain access to further information by calling your local newspaper, or contact:

Gloria Talamas
Stock Market Game Director
120 Broadway, 35th Floor
New York, NY 10271
(212) 608-0519 at www.smgww.org

You simply can't miss with this integrative activity. Kids love it and learn so much!

10

SNOWFLAKES

Rosemary Callard-Szulgit

What could be more intriguing to a child than discovering the mystery of a snowflake? The development of snowflakes provides a fascinating study in crystal formation, a combination of science and mathematics.

For her creativity project last semester, one of my graduate students chose to teach us how to make paper snowflakes. Colleen Close presented the idea that students enter our classrooms with many common traits. We spend the year spinning teacher magic and creativity with each child and the myriad of beautiful and unique "products" ten months later can be astounding!

Here are the "snowflake steps" for you to use in your own classrooms to develop this same analogy—and create beautiful winter decorations at the same time.

TO MAKE A SNOWFLAKE

1. With a square piece of paper, fold it in half diagonally.

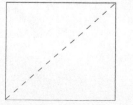 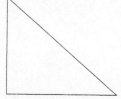

2. Fold the triangle in half and crease at the midpoint, then open the triangle again.

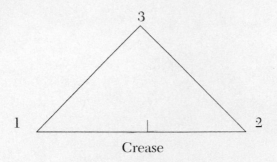

3. Fold corners 1 and 2 up and at an angle so they cross and completely cover each other.

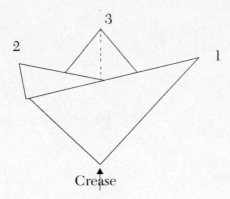

4. Fold in half so curves 1 and 2 meet.

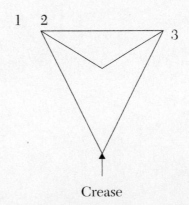

5. Begin by cutting off the tip at the crease. Then cut a design in the top. (Do not cut above the dotted line below.)

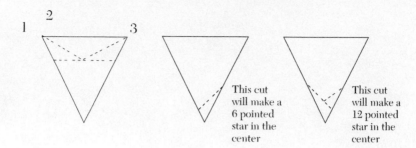

This cut will make a 6 pointed star in the center

This cut will make a 12 pointed star in the center

STEM

Rosemary Callard-Szulgit

Science, technology, engineering, and mathematics (STEM) are the four areas where the Directorate for Education and Human Resources of the National Science Foundation is seeking to broaden the participation of girls and women. Research, dissemination of research, and integration of proven good practices in education that will lead to a better diversity in the workplace are the major goals of STEM. Service proposals may request up to $500,000 each year for five years, contributing to the knowledge base addressing gender-related differences in learning and in the educational experiences that affect student interest, performance and choice of careers.

Contact Ruta Sevo, Program Director, Division of Human Resource Development, 4201 Wilson Blvd., Rm. 815, N. Arlington, VA 22230.

II

SCIENCE ACTIVITIES

⑫

CHEMISTRY OLYMPIAD

Rosemary Callard-Szulgit

Any time I can encourage and/or include my students in an academic competition, I jump at the chance. I love the time and study investment in a healthy competition, and the U.S. National Chemistry Olympiad (USNCO) is just that. Interested students begin with local exams in March where nominees are selected for the national exam. Local sections select their nominees by various means, including the USNCO local section exam, a locally prepared exam, laboratory practicals, teacher recommendations, and/or other regional events with competitive activities among school teams. Former exam copies may be accessed for study on the web at http://nhb.topcities.com/Chemclub/olympiads.html.

In April, sponsored by the ACS (American Chemical Society), the local area winners proceed to a national exam of a two-hour multiple choice and a two-hour written response exam. A two-week study camp is supported every June leading into the International Chemistry Olympiad in July. Top winners receive gold medals, followed by silver medals and finally, diplomas of excellence to the remaining contestants. Future international competitions will be held in the following countries: Korea (2006), Lithuania (2007), Hungary (2008), and England (2009).

Competitions such as the U.S. National Chemistry Olympiad continue to encourage excellence in our outstanding science students, while helping them understand and compete in the local, national, and international arenas. I believe this is an invaluable plus for our children in our increasingly competitive business world—and winners enjoy the pleasure of travel and exciting cultural experiences as well!

⓭

CHALLENGER CENTER FOR SPACE SCIENCE EDUCATION: SPACE DAY 2005 DESIGN CHALLENGES

Rosemary Callard-Szulgit

Each year, the Challenger Center for Space Science Education produces an educational initiative, emphasizing collaborative learning and academic excellence in science, math, and technology. For 2005, the inquiry-based learning tool theme was "Return to the Moon." Winning teams are selected by a committee of education experts. Celebration prizes in 2005 included an invitation to Washington, D.C., for the Space Day national celebration, where members of the winning teams participated in a recognition ceremony.

For yearly details and registration forms, visit the Internet at www.spaceday.com.

THE CUTTING EDGE

Greg Szulgit

This exercise can have profound effects on students. The personal contact at the end is important because it exposes the human behind the big ideas. Often, the details that the student remembers about such an encounter are more influential than the academic problem of interest. In a best-case scenario, the student will adopt a view of the researcher as less of a celebrity and more of a role model.

Science and math textbooks are full of information that we pack into our skulls, but we sometimes forget where the information comes from. Remember that information was not always known; somebody had to discover it. In this exercise, the student will track down a researcher who is discovering new things about the world—things that have never, in the history of humankind, been known before! The student can do this any number of ways, but I have outlined some steps below that might make the process easier.

1. Find "the cutting edge" of a field of interest. One of the easiest ways to do this is to have the student type the word "research" into a search engine such as Google, followed by his or her topic of interest (examples in science are easy: "horses," "Mars," "robots"; math is a bit trickier because you may need to know a specific topic such as "Fibonocci sequences"). The student may need to poke around a bit, but should be able to come up with a website for a university or some other research organization.
2. Have the student try to answer these questions based on what he or she finds:

    a) Who is doing this research and where are they located?
    b) What basic questions are these people trying to answer?
    c) Why are these questions especially important and interesting?

3. If this topic is interesting to the student, have him or her look around at related sites to gather more information about the topic. Keep looking around until the student feels that he or she understands the topic fairly well.

4. Have the student contact one of the scientists or mathematicians who is doing the work. Often, there will be contact information on the website. Have the student introduce himself or herself and tell the subject of their research that they are interested in their work and want to learn more about it. Ultimately, it would be ideal if the student could pay them a visit in their lab or office. If the student wants to, he or she can come up with a few questions ahead of time to ask them such as:

    a) How did they become interested in the topic?
    b) What do they think are the most important unanswered questions in science today?
    c) What is their favorite aspect of their research?
    d) Did they enjoy school when they were your age?
    e) Do they enjoy hobbies outside of their work?

There are also plenty of places on the Internet that allow anyone to post questions to experts in a field. This can be a fun way to get a personalized answer to a question that intrigues the student, who will often be learning about what is known (as opposed to learning about the areas of knowledge that are unexplored—see the difference?). For sites that allow the public to ask an expert, check out those that are listed at www.cln.org/int_expert.html.

15

HURRICANE HUNTERS

Rosemary Callard-Szulgit

Interested students can now "get on board" a hurricane hunter mission of the Aircraft Operations Center by visiting www.aoc.noaa.gov. This center is part of the National Oceanic and Atmospherics Administration's Marine and Aviation Office, coordinating scientific investigations into the eye of hurricanes. Studies of acid rain, soil erosion, and marine animal populations are just a few of their many fascinating topics of investigative value.

16

THE INTEL SCIENCE TALENT SEARCH

Rosemary Callard-Szulgit

The Intel Science Talent Search, previously known as the Westinghouse Science Talent Search, is America's oldest precollege science contest. Eligible students include high school seniors in the United States and its territories, and American students attending school abroad. Each year, almost 2,000 students accept the challenge of completing an entry for the Intel Science Talent Search, with finalists competing for the top prize of a $100,000 scholarship. Each student completes a written description of his or her research, plus an entry form that encourages student creativity and interest in science. Search candidates are judged by a board of ten distinguished scientists from a variety of disciplines. The top 300 entrants are selected as semifinalists. Intel and Science Service recommend these students to colleges and universities for admission and financial assistance. Top contenders are announced in January with final judging in March. Next, forty finalists are selected from the 300 semifinalists. Both groups are announced separately in January. For more information, write Science Service, 1719 N. St. NW, Washington, DC 20036; (202) 785-2255; fax (202) 785-1243; or visit www.sciserv.org.contact.asp.

17

THE JASON EXPEDITION

Rosemary Callard-Szulgit
Greg Szulgit

The JASON Expedition is an excellent, nonprofit, nationwide educational program sponsored by the JASON Foundation for Education, whose primary goal is to get kids in grades 5–8 excited about science, mathematics, and technology. It emphasizes hands-on and interdisciplinary learning by providing real-time contact with current scientific research and researchers. Supported by NASA, NOAA, and the U.S. Department of Education, it can be used as a supplement or a foundation of science and math programs.

Each year, the JASON Expedition designs a new curriculum around a theme based on an ecosystem. They then approach this theme from a variety of angles, weaving together writing, math, science, and social science. From this point of view, it is the best written curriculum that we have ever seen. Furthermore, JASON's creators cater to education standards and have online advice that shows teachers how they can use the curriculum to "teach to the test." This is one of the most important features of JASON, as it provides a way for the program to be a *time-saver* as opposed to a *time drain*. The last thing educators need is "one more thing to do," but JASON can actually help reduce one's work load *while* teaching to the test! Of course, some time and energy will be involved with "shifting gears" if a teacher has a curriculum already established, but we think that you will find it worth the initial effort.

The activities are widely varied, but all tie in to the central theme for that particular year's JASON Expedition. Throughout the curriculum, students are encouraged to interact with other JASON students around the world and with the JASON Expedition scientists through various online technologies. They also interact with "Student Argonauts" (a diverse range of students who have been chosen to be part of the scientific expeditions being studied). The program culminates in a live broadcast that is delivered at a primary interactive network site (PINS) where the students interact in real time via telepresence with the scientists and Student Argonauts. Students and teachers can also view the live broadcast via live webcast in their classrooms.

To join an expedition, teachers purchase an annual JASON curriculum and can choose to attend a live broadcast at one of the PINS in their area. The PINS costs are quite reasonable and will vary by region. In Cleveland, for example, the 2006 program is partially subsidized with a cost of only $125 per classroom (the curriculum would be $359 otherwise). The teachers then adapt the curriculum to fit their particular classroom needs using some or all of the JASON activities. As previously mentioned, these activities emphasize science and technology, but also have strong history, literature, and social science components.

Key points for a successful JASON Expedition are:

1. The JASON Expedition will not work by simply placing technology into classrooms or by bringing students to a live broadcast. It is of the utmost importance that teachers build the students' excitement by using the curriculum prior to attending the live broadcast. Students then arrive at the PINS primed to have an exciting experience. Buildup is important. As an example of this concept, imagine walking down a city street on a Sunday afternoon and seeing a building with a pole on the top. This pole pierces a discoball-like sphere, which slides down the pole as you watch curiously. Would you feel a thrill? Probably not. Yet millions of people watch the ball drop in Times Square each New Year's Eve and get very excited! It becomes a memorable experience for them because they have prepared themselves for something special.

2. Teachers should try to incorporate local opportunities into the JASON curriculum, especially if they are not close enough to a PINS to make the trip to the live broadcast. The curriculum can be easily correlated to teachers' existing activities or lessons be-

cause of JASON's multidisciplinary approach. Field trips to art museums can have just as much to do with the JASON Expedition as contact with local scientists.

DOES IT WORK?

The Center for Children and Technology, a nonprofit consulting organization in Washington (http://main.edc.org), has evaluated the JASON program for the last three years and compiled data from surveys that were administered to JASON participants. One of the conclusions in their third-year report states that,

> Our work has shown that the JASON Expedition, comprised of an interdisciplinary, multimedia science curriculum, not only engaged diverse students in science learning in ways that students themselves found more powerful than the typical science classroom, but also taught students 21st century skills. Most importantly, the curriculum broadened students' perspectives about what constitutes scientific experimentation and exploration, what real scientists are like, and the value of learning science in their own lives. These aspects of learning science in the upper elementary and middle grades are important, and supply a critical link between diverse groups of students and the field of science. The evaluation substantiated teachers' claims about the positive impact of JMSC materials on their students. Moreover, our research over the last three years has consistently shown that JASON curricular materials engage different types of students and teachers. In addition, as we showed in the discussion section, these findings are supported by the bodies of literature in scientific literacy for all as well as learning environments and teacher quality." (Goldenberg et al. 2003)

The JASON Foundation continues to win multiple awards annually. In 2004, their curriculum, *Rainforests at the Crossroads*, was given the award for Excellence for "Best Science Product" by *Teachology & Learning* magazine.

Based on our own experience with the program, we can confidently say that it is a superb example of progressive thinking in education, which is why we have decided to dedicate several pages of our book to the JASON Expedition.

THE 2005–2006 CURRICULUM: MYSTERIES OF
EARTH AND MARS

We have included information specific to the 2005–2006 curriculum, which focuses on the exploration and comparison of Mars and Earth. Using this program, students will work online with an ethnically diverse group of male and female scientists from NASA's headquarters, Jet Propulsion Laboratory, and Ames Research Center, as well as from Arizona State University and the University of Hawaii. Experiments in the classroom will help students explore the multiple research topics, which include:

- How do engineers build robotic rovers to meet the grueling conditions of Mars?
- How do the many systems of Mars Reconnaissance Orbiter work smoothly together?
- What can we learn from studying craters on Earth and Mars?
- What can Martian meteorites tell us about Mars?
- How does the study of extreme places on Earth help us better understand if life could exist on Mars?
- How can studying modern microbial systems help us search for signs of life on Mars?

Table 17.1 shows how the curriculum correlates to National Science Education Standards.

Table 17.1

Unit 1: Physical Science	National Science Education Standards
Examines the physical properties of space science as well as the engineering challenges of robotic exploration. Topics include: • Characteristic properties and chemical changes of water: freezing point, boiling point, solubility, density, chemical reactions • Motions and Forces: Newton's Laws, gravity • Transfer of Energy: potential and kinetic energy • Science and Technology: technological design	• B.1 Properties and Changes in Matter • B.2 Motion and Forces • B.3 Transfer of Energy • D.1 Water Cycle • D.3 Earth in the Solar System • E.1 Abilities of Technological Design

Unit 2: Earth and Space Science	National Science Education Standards
Examines comparative planetology, the geological features and processes on Earth and Mars. Topics include: • Physical Geology: landforms, rocks, minerals, and soil • Geological Processes: tectonics, volcanism, cratering, erosion, and measuring geological time • Electromagnetism: waves, infrared radiation, and spectroscopy • Solar System: planets and meteors	• A.1 Abilities Necessary to do Scientific Inquiry • A.2 Process of Scientific Inquiry • B.1 Properties and Changes in Matter • D.1 Structure of the Earth System • D.2 Earth's History

Unit 3: Life Science	National Science Education Standards
Examines requirements for life, astrobiology (the search for life throughout the solar system) and extremophiles (organisms adapted to extreme environments). Topics include: • Requirements for Life: energy, nutrients, water • Living Systems: structure and function in living systems, cells, microbes • Diversity and Adaptation of Organisms: extreme environments, extremophiles • Earth's History: fossils, biosignatures	• A Science as Inquiry • B.1 Properties and Changes in Matter • C.1 Structure and Function of Living Systems • C.3 Regulation and Behavior • C.4 Population and Ecosystems • C.5 Diversity and Adaptations of Organisms • D Earth and Space Science • E Science and Technology • G History and Nature of Science

18

LIFE MIGHT BE OUT THERE . . .

Greg Szulgit

If you are looking for intelligent life in the rest of the universe, you are not alone. In fact, you can join others in the search! The SETI@home project helps regular people like you and me join in one of the most ambitious projects of all time to search for traces of other civilizations. Download the software from the SETI@home site (http://setiathome.s-sl.berkeley.edu) and your computer will process data while you are not using it (this is called "parallel computing" and is explained at the site). Happy hunting!

While scientists do not expect to find any unknown civilizations in our own solar system, we are presently exploring several places to see if some type of life might be hidden close by. This new field is called astrobiology and it is a serious endeavor. Some of the places being explored include Mars, the moons of Jupiter and Saturn, and the insides of comets! What might life look like on another planet? Will it be any bigger than bacteria? Will it be made of the same chemicals as life on Earth is? Some people believe that life did not develop on Earth but was carried here inside meteors. Could there be meteors full of single-celled life zipping around our solar system?

To answer some of these questions, visit some of the sites listed below. While you are there, you can also check out tons of information about the space programs of the United States and other countries.

Sites for kids include:

http://education.nasa.gov/home/index.html

http://kids.msfc.nasa.gov/
www.nasa.gov/audience/forkids/home/

Sites for older students include some basic information on the Centennial Challenge, where NASA will give literally millions of dollars to groups that come up with the best design ideas for new spacecraft:
http://exploration.nasa.gov/
http://exploration.nasa.gov/centennialchallenge

Also, try typing "astrobiology" into your favorite search engine to see what you turn up. You will be fascinated by the results!

19

MARBLE MACHINES

Greg Szulgit

These are classic fun, and get students accustomed to combining artistry with physics. The task is simple but can become as elaborate as students desire: make a chute that allows a ball (marble) to roll through an adventure of sorts. One way to stimulate ideas is to collect lots of material before you have any idea what it will be used for. Having the building materials around you will inspire ideas that you had never considered. Some ideas that folks might want to include to spice things up:

1. a jump
2. a randomizing section where marbles can go down one of several paths with equal frequency (not easy)
3. a section where the active marble activates other marbles
4. a section where the marble pauses for a certain amount of time and then proceeds without any input from the person running the machine
5. a counter that advances each time a marble passes by
6. the inclusion of a household object
7. a practical function (in other words, it does something useful)
8. the inclusion of music in some way

It's always nice to add artistic touches to the machine. When you build yours, send me a picture at szulgit2@aol.com; I would love to see it! ☺

One of the greatest examples that I have seen of such a "virtual" machine can be found at www.nanahiro.com/compe/main.html. If the site address is not functioning, you may be able to track down a version by typing "Treasure Box" into your favorite search engine.

A similar type of machine (although not usually involving marbles) is a "Rube Goldberg device." Check out this neat example in the form of a two-minute car commercial: http://multimedia.honda-eu.com/accord/index.html. Once you are there, you will have to wade through a bit of advertisement until you can download a copy of the movie. It might be easier to simply type "Honda Accord Rube Goldberg" into a search engine such as Google and then look around at the sites that appear.

If you get excited by what you see, then why not design your own device and enter the national Rube Goldberg Machine Contest held each year by the National Student Engineering Organization at Purdue University? Rules can be found at:

www.rube-goldberg.com/html/contest.htm.

20

NATURE'S ARTFUL ARCHITECTURE

Greg Szulgit

Find a plant, a branch, or even just a few leaves. Their shape and structure are truly amazing and beautiful, yet the patterns that compose them are sometimes deceptively simple. This exercise focuses on honing a student's powers of observation.

1. Look at your plant or plant part for one second and then turn away and draw it for one minute without looking again. How did you do? Did you get the details right?
2. Now look at the plant for 30 seconds before turning away to draw it a second time for a minute. Notice how much better your drawing was the second time. You looked at the plant for only 30 seconds, which is not much, and you were able to fill in quite a bit of detail. How often do we simply glance at the world and its objects for only a second or two? What would your perception be like if you took 30 seconds now and then to really examine the detail that surrounds you?
3. Every plant, and structure within that plant, has a unique shape that is often composed of a few simple patterns (this is owed partially to the timing of certain events as the plant grows). If you can get some precise measuring equipment, measure the distances and dimensions of the elements that dictate the pattern (for example, how far is it between needles? how far between branches? how far until each branch splits into two or more?). Can you dis-

cover some of the simple rules that lead to an overall pattern? How would you describe these rules?

For an extra challenge, try graphing the measurements that you made. You might see patterns emerging in a graph that you did not realize earlier.

21

PINHOLE CAMERAS

Rosemary Callard-Szulgit

Being fellow Rochesterians, it is with pleasure we include this Eastman Kodak activity supporting the making and operation of pinhole cameras: www.pinhole.com/resources/pinhole126/pinhole.htm.

This site includes complete instructions for making your own camera, including illustrations and listing of required materials. Instructions for loading film and using the camera are also included, along with photos actually taken by pinhole cameras!

㉒

SCIENCE OLYMPIAD

Rosemary Callard-Szulgit

I have always entered my students in as many competitions, such as the Olympiads, as I could throughout my thirty-seven-year career! Why? Because they foster teamwork; individual responsibility; creative thinking; possible county, state, national, and international competitions; exposure to other students' thinking at their own age levels; seeing other age-division products; and thinking outside of the box and routines. It can be very easy to fall into in our own little routines in our home school districts, no matter how good we are or think we are!

Science Olympiads (www.soinc.org/informat.htm) serve to foster the three main goals of science concepts and knowledge, science processes and thinking skills, and science application and technology. Events support scientific knowledge (factual information) and science processes and the skills of application.

Teams are composed of fifteen students, which prepare throughout the year for competition in the Olympiads held at the local, state, and national competitions. Topics in biology, earth science, physics, technology, chemistry, and problem solving are included.

There is a small fee to cover a copy of the Science Olympiad manual for coaches and the official rules. Awards are given for each event and championship trophies are awarded to the Division B (grades 6–9) and Division C (grades 9–12).

23

SCIENCE TOY MAKER

Rosemary Callard-Szulgit

With handy links to explanations of scientific concepts at work, the Science Toy Maker site (www.sciencetoymaker.org) entices all who enjoy the mystery that toys exude in the investigative sciences. Projects for all student levels are available with easy-to-follow instructions. Related links for the scientific explanations at work in each toy are available, along with other related links.

This could be a marvelous site/activity for all children with the mystery to learn, create, and have fun!

24

SPACE DAY—101 WAYS TO CELEBRATE

Rosemary Callard-Szulgit

Teachers and students can easily access the Space Day website (www .spaceday.org) to gain loads of activities pertaining to the galaxy, cosmos, and atmosphere. Each year a different theme is developed with interactive themes. A free, downloadable PDF file is available at the website by visiting "News and events/this just in." Happy space trails to you!

25

TINY WORLDS

Greg Szulgit

Most animals and fungi (and some plants) are much smaller than we are, so it is easy for us to overlook many of the important factors that affect life for these creatures. The purpose of this exercise is to get students thinking about the concept of tiny habitats. The closer they look, the more they will be able to find tiny habitats that exist within other habitats. Think about a patch of grass, for example: we might think that it is just one habitat—but when you look closely, you will find that there are lots of tiny environments in just that one small area. The dirt might be cool and damp, while the top of the grass might be dry and warm. The stems of the grass are under the leaves, or blades, and are often in the shade, while the leaves themselves might be exposed to strong sunlight all day long.

The assignment is for the students to find an outdoor space of their own choosing that is approximately the size of their hand. They should begin by drawing this space in detail (using colored pencils). The drawing should take them quite some time, as they should record every detail possible. The more time they spend observing the details, the more they will appreciate the tiny little world within this space. As they draw their space, they should consider the following parameters and how those parameters change from one tiny space to the next:

- light
- heat
- water/moisture

- fresh air
- food
- colors
- any other parameters that they can think of (like movement of the surroundings)

Now they should describe several mini-environments that they have found within this area (e.g., they might describe the underside of a leaf as one environment, while the top side of the leaf is a very different environment; in what ways do they differ?). They should dedicate a paragraph to each parameter or mini-environment.

Finally, they should spend a few paragraphs describing all of the creatures (not just the animals) that are present. Why do they think those creatures are located where they are, and how do they think each creature deals with its mini-environment? How do they suppose the various creatures interact with each other?

As usual, both teachers and students might want to modify the assignment a bit to fulfill their own interests.

26

TREE OF LIFE

Greg Szulgit

This exercise is meant to familiarize you with the very basic aspects of the Tree of Life Web Project. It is a project that makes information accessible regarding all known creatures and their relationships to each other. The "tree" is called a "phylogenetic tree" and it is our best understanding of the evolutionary relationships between all creatures. Following the steps below, your assignment is to choose a creature at random and answer some questions about it.

1. Go to http://tolweb.org.
2. Think of whatever creature you can and perform a search for that creature (find the "search" link).
3. Once you have found your creature, create an entire lineage for that creature by selecting the "containing group" for each level and by writing down the previous level. Continue this until you have your creature traced back to the kingdom level. If you can note which levels are the phylum, class, order, family, genus, and species, then you should do so. In many cases there will be several steps in between some of the levels; write them down, but don't worry about identifying them as "super" or "sub" groups (e.g., many orders have super-orders and/or sub-orders that go with them).
4. The phylogenetic tree for your creature is based on scientific evidence that has been published in a scientific journal. Look for a reference to this publication (it will probably be below the tree).

In that publication, the scientists will explain why they believe that the creatures are related as shown in the diagram.

5. What is your creature like? What is something interesting that you did not already know? To do this you might need to go to other sources on the Internet (see the section for links toward the bottom of the page). Of the Internet pages that you looked at, which one seemed most helpful?

6. Poke around on the Tree of Life site; it's really interesting!

For a list of cool creatures, try some of these:
Beroida
Slimoniidae
Trichoplax adhaerens
Eutardigrada
Peripatidae
Symbion pandora
Fenestrata
Neomyxine
Porphyroglossum
Desmidiaceae
Euascomycetes
Auriculariales

III

TECHNOLOGY/BUSINESS OPPORTUNITIES

27

GIRLS GO TECH

Rosemary Callard-Szulgit

Girlsgotech.org (www.girlsgotech.org) is a wonderful resource of activities intended for girls and their parents/teachers to access creative ideas and support in the areas of science, math, and technology.

Most girls have lost interest in math, science, and technology by the age of twelve. This initiative encourages girls to develop an early interest in these subjects to help ensure a more diverse, dynamic, and productive work force in our country's future. Sponsored by the Girl Scouts of the U.S.A., girls are introduced to mathematics as the exciting algebra that NASA uses to plot a rocket's path to Mars, rather than the arithmetic of adding, subtracting, multiplying, and dividing that girls are so often used to thinking of.

Technology is emphasized as a useful tool of linking girls through cell phones, the Internet, instant messaging, MP3 players, and sports cars, to name just a few. Science, as we know it, is all around us!

Girlsgotech has three interesting games to explore and try, some of which may be suitable for boys as well.

1. "Mandala," meaning center or circle, lets the reader make her or his own kaleidoscope
2. "Think about Thinking" helps the reader understand mixed messages, such as the brain using two different pathways to discern seeing a color while reading the word.
3. "Sound of Science" helps the reader compose her own digital music.

Girlsgotech also highlights successful women whose careers are in science, mathematics, and technology, thus providing excellent role models for young girls. It provides information on some exciting careers, a resource section, and tips for parents in the Girls Go Tech booklet provided.

After clicking on one of the site's fun buttons, I learned that I am 1,829,088,000 seconds old! Why not calculate how many seconds old you are, then go to www.girlsgotech.org and check your calculations while you enjoy this wonderful support system for girls in technology, math, and science?

Girls Go Tech can also be reached through the Girl Scouts of the U.S.A. at 420 Fifth Avenue, New York, NY 10018, phone (800) GSUSA 4 U.

28

LET'S GET REAL

Rosemary Callard-Szulgit

Let's Get Real (www.LGReal.org) is a wonderful national academic competition providing all participating students an opportunity to work on teams and gain experience with real business challenges. Corporate sponsors supply real challenges for which teams submit solutions in business format. Each team chooses from a list of challenges the one it finds most interesting, including areas such as environmental issues, manufacturing, distribution, software creation, human resources, chemistry, health and safety, facilities design, public relations, engineering, or any other areas deemed important to the corporations involved.

Let's Get Real is a 501(c)(3) not-for-profit corporation, and the following information is reprinted with their permission. There is no entry fee for students or schools. How can you lose? This academic competition provides today's students with the opportunity of choices, application of interests, teamwork, real-world applications, creativity, problem-solving skills, and who knows, maybe even future job employment or positive connection with a corporation whose challenge was selected for competition.

RULES AND REGISTRATION

Introduction

Let's Get Real is a competition that gives young students the opportunity to solve real-life issues faced by the sponsoring corporations and provides corporate sponsors with the opportunity to meet talented students. For questions or comments, contact your state coordinator or program coordinator.

Team Eligibility

All sixth- through twelfth-grade students from any school are eligible. Students do not have to be affiliated with a school setting to participate . . . in other words, home schooling, Boy or Girl Scouts, neighborhood friends, and so forth can form teams with an adult coordinator. Students may work on any of the problems. All entries *must* be by teams. *No* individual entries will be considered. Teams must be no smaller than two and no larger than six students. Members of the team may be from the same or different grade levels and may be from the same or different schools. Each team must have at least one adult coordinator.

Adult Coordinator

The team's adult coordinator must be at least twenty-one years old, be able to provide guidance and direction to the students, and serve as the primary contact with Let's Get Real. A coordinator may sponsor more than one team.

Registration and Contact Forms

Each team must submit a separate *registration form* and *contract form*. Each team may work on more than one problem. However, a separate registration form should be submitted for each problem. The contract form may be duplicated so each team member can submit a separate form for convenience. In addition, a student may be a member of more than one team.

Solving the Problems

The solution must be developed by the students. Parents, teachers, adult coordinators, and other nonteam members may provide training, guidance, transportation, and other indirect assistance only.

Select one or more problems from the sponsor's problem list. Submit a separate registration form and contract form for each problem and for each team. Each entry will be initially judged based on the team's written report. The written report must meet the following requirements (refer also to The Judging Process to see exactly what will be evaluated):

- All assumptions made in arriving at the solution must be clearly stated.
- The costs and benefits of the suggested solution must be clearly stated.
- The written report must be typed and must not exceed ten double-spaced pages (using 12-point type and 1-inch margins).

Document all the resources used in arriving at your solution. This includes the time (hours) and money spent. This documentation of expenses is not for reimbursement, but it will be considered in determining the cost-effectiveness of your work as it relates to the quality of your solution.

Diagrams, drawings, or illustrations and computer simulations or models are acceptable as appendices to the written report and will not be counted in the page limit. In addition, you may prepare audio or videotapes, models, or other material helpful to understanding the written report (this material will *not* be returned unless the team is selected for the final oral presentation). However, please note that only finalists selected on the basis of the initial submission will be given an opportunity to make an oral presentation. Therefore, material that requires an accompanying presentation (e.g., 35-mm slides) should be prepared only if the team is invited for an oral presentation.

Submitting Solutions

Please send *all* completed registration forms, contract forms, and solution by or before the deadline for the specific challenge to:

Let's Get Real
624 Waltonville Road
Hummelstown, PA 17036

THE JUDGING PROCESS

Judging will be done by a panel of employees from the corporate sponsor. Each corporate sponsor will judge solutions to its own problems using the following scoring sheet (rubric developed by Myron E. Yoder, M.Ed., social studies curriculum coordinator at Allentown School District and adjunct professor of education at Cedar Crest College). The written solutions will be judged according to the following criteria:

Practicality or Implementation Potential (10 points). The solution is practical and could be implemented with existing technology.

Effectiveness of the Solution (20 points). The written report is clear, concise, and "sells" the idea. Also, the report meets the style guidelines, is neat and well documented, and is easy to follow.

Cost and Benefit of the Solution (20 points). The cost of the solution is clearly documented, and the benefit of the solution is clearly documented and stated. Also, the analysis of the cost/benefit of the solution is reasonable and understandable.

Creativity and Originality (20 points). The solution is creative and demonstrates thinking beyond the conventional and obvious. The solution also demonstrates ideas developed solely by the group.

Development of the Idea (10 points). There is a chronological log discussion about how your idea was formed, developed, and finally acted on by your group. You may use a narrative in place of a log.

Documentation of the Development of the Solution (20 points). All work and expenses must be clearly documented and appended to the end of the written report. The documentation must be clearly presented and easily understood, and it must be presented in an organized and neat fashion.

ORAL PRESENTATION

Finalists will be invited *at their own expense* to the appropriate corporate sponsor's location for an oral presentation. Finalists will be questioned by the judges to determine originality of the idea, knowledge of the subject, and ability to communicate and sell the idea clearly and succinctly. The oral presentation should be limited to fifteen minutes, followed by about ten minutes of questioning by the judges. If your team is invited to the finals, please feel free to employ a PowerPoint presentation.

29

The PPG Industries Foundation

Rosemary Callard-Szulgit

I love grant opportunities such as this from the PPG Industries Foundation (www.ppg.com)! It favors projects that promote academic excellence and support for students of high academic achievement and programs that attract young people to the studies of science. The foundation's vision is to support the next generation of leaders in business, science, and technology. Deadline is open and no limit to funding is mentioned. How can you go wrong in applying?

IV

STILL MORE ACTIVITIES

30

ACADEMIC DECATHLON AND NORTHRUP CORPORATION

Rosemary Callard-Szulgit

While the Academic Decathlon is a scholastic competition in the ten categories of math, science, economics, essay, social studies, speech, fine arts, language and literature, interview, and a Super Quiz, we wanted to include it in this book because it supports the high standards of academic achievement and creates partnerships with local corporations and service organizations. Plus, we always love the potential financial benefits to the student winners!

The decathlon is for teams of high school students consisting of nine members each. Competitions begin at the local level, with winning teams proceeding to the regional, state, and finally national levels.

Three levels of awards can be earned in each category along the way—bronze, silver, and gold. Champion teams and individual winners are recognized with huge financial scholarships awarded by the Northrup Corporation at the national competitions, starting with $2,000 to individual bronze medal winners up to $30,000 to overall gold, silver, and bronze winners.

For further information, e-mail info@usad.org.

③①

CAN'T YOU SIT STILL?

Greg Szulgit and Karl Szulgit

How fast are you going right now, even if you are sitting down? It sounds simple, but stop and think about it for a bit. Did you consider that the Earth is spinning? Now start thinking on a bigger scale. Think of all the ways in which you are moving. Got your answer? Did you consider each of these?

1. You are standing on a piece of the Earth's crust that is moving due to plate tectonics (probably less than an inch per year).
2. The Earth is spinning at one rotation per day, and the speed at which you are moving on its surface depends on your latitude (think about it).
3. The Earth is moving around the sun once per year.
4. The sun is one of about *100 billion* other stars in the Milky Way Galaxy. All of these stars are spinning around the center like a pinwheel.
5. The Milky Way is one of *hundreds of billions* of other galaxies that are moving through space at an incredibly fast (and accelerating!) rate from the center of our universe.
6. Is there anything beyond our known universe? Are we in just one of many universes, with all of them moving around each other? That one is still an open question . . .

Even if you had all of these in your answer, did you take into account that each of the atoms that you are made of is zipping around or vibrating intensely inside of your body (this is called Brownian motion)?

So, the next time somebody says to you, "Can't you sit still?" you can simply tell them, "Nope."

For more amazing information about our universe, go to www .windows.ucar.edu.

32

CLASSROOM EARTH AND ENVIRONMENTAL EDUCATION

Rosemary Callard-Szulgit

Descriptive information on how teachers can obtain the best and most usable environmental programs available today can now be accessed at Classroom Earth, www.classroomearth.org. Thanks to the National Environmental Education and Training Foundation, K–12 teachers, parents, students, and community members may access this new and free website, which includes a collection of top-notch programs, descriptions, reviews, and useful information on how to obtain materials and training in conjunction with environmental education.

This site would be especially valuable during the month of April when classrooms throughout the country celebrate and actively support Earth Day!

33

EXPLORER SCHOOLS AND NASA

Rosemary Callard-Szulgit

Explorer Schools provides a wonderful opportunity for student in grades 4 through 9 to work with education specialists from NASA Centers on science and mathematics instruction. Each year, schools nationwide are eligible to apply online to become one of fifty new NASA Explorer School teams in a three-year partnership. The teams consist of education administrators and teachers, with a focus on bringing engaging mathematics and science learning to students. An additional benefit to participating as one of the fifty Explorer Schools is the acquisition of new technology tools and teaching resources, using NASA's content, experts, and many other valuable resources.

To apply online, go to www.explorerschools.nasa.gov. What an exceptional opportunity this provides for our gifted and all interested students!

34

INTERNET CHESS CLUB

Rosemary Callard-Szulgit

InstantChess.com (at www.instantchess.com/school) is an Internet chess club based in Moscow that provides school chess clubs an opportunity to learn and compete with other school chess clubs around the world. For further information, write to:

InstantChess USA
P.O. Box 90636
Austin, TX 78709-0636

INVERSIONS

Greg Szulgit

As a largely visual thinker, I remember puzzling over this concept in eighth grade. Hopefully, your students will find it as intriguing as I did.

In the picture below, there is a diamond placed inside a square. If I were to fold the outer shape (the square) around the inner shape, I would get a new picture, as shown:

What would the results look like if I placed other shapes inside the square?

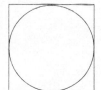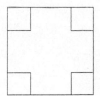

Now try to diagram them all in three dimensions (an example shown here):

Invent your own!

- Even Gifted Students Sometimes Lose Their Heads.

36

MIT INVENTEAMS

Rosemary Callard-Szulgit

Fifteen schools nationwide will be awarded grants up to $10,000 each to create a problem-solving invention. High school teachers throughout the country can apply in the spring. A panel of Massachusetts Institute of Technology faculty and alumni, professional inventors, and engineers and Lemelson-MIT Program staff will review the applications. In the fall, thirty-five finalists will be invited to complete a second application, which will include details about the proposed invention, the team's plan for completing the work, and a budget estimate. Interested educators may gain grant information at www.inventeams.org.

Science, math, and technology teachers from public, private, charter, and vocational high schools can apply for a grant to develop an invention as an in-class or extracurricular project.

Winning schools/students will work on their inventions during the following year. Bravo and thank you to the prestigious Lemelson-MIT Inventeams for this grant opportunity in the sciences!

A WALK IN THE WOODS

Rosemary Callard-Szulgit

This website activity is designed for urban children in grades 3 through 5 who would otherwise not have opportunities to visits the woods. Developed by the University of Illinois Extension, this virtual walk in the woods may by accessed at www.urbanext.uiuc.edu/woods/index.html. Students can click on various icons and learn about plants and animals they might see on their "walk." Precautions and trail etiquette are available as an introductory lesson.

A teacher's guide is included to enrich classroom use. What a marvelous way to help urban children enjoy the woods in all their splendor! Thanks, University of Illinois!

V

ACADEMIC ENVIRONS

38

DUKE UNIVERSITY TALENT
IDENTIFICATION PROGRAM (TIP)

Rosemary Callard-Szulgit

I have long had respect and admiration for Duke University. When our daughter applied and was accepted in their Medical Pathology Assistant Program, I couldn't have been happier. While visiting the N.C. School of Science and Mathematics and Moss Meadow, I also took the time to visit Duke TIP, and was given a very cordial welcome from Kristen Stephens and Bobbie Collins-Perry, editor and coeditor of their Duke newsletter. The beautiful and newly renovated historic building was bustling with dedicated and committed staff members. I tried not to become overwhelmed with the multitude of programs, activities, scholarships, research, advanced placements, summer study programs, and weekend adventures, just to name a few of the boundless opportunities this organization provides!

Founded in 1980 through a grant from the Duke Endowment, the Duke Talent Identification Program (www.tip.duke.edu) is a leader in identifying academically talented students and providing innovative programs to support their optimal educational development. Over one million students have benefited from one or more of TIP's unique and exciting programs since its inception in 1980!

TIP's Summer Residential Program now hosts over 80,000 seventh-grade students annually at Duke and other locations around the country. Nearly 35,000 students participate annually in the fourth- and fifth-grade talent search! Duke TIP Summer Studies and Precollegiate Programs challenge students with fast-paced course across the liberal arts curriculum and in special programs in science and business. There are also International Precollegiate sites. TIP also offers a Leadership Institute. Also, high schools students may study alongside Duke undergraduates in the second summer school session for Duke University credit. Duke has also begun a series of new programs during the academic year to serve a broader spectrum of students.

Scholar Weekends are especially intriguing to me. Geared for academically talented students in grades 8–11, the weekend courses might include law, writing, business, environmental issues, philosophy, medicine and drama. Since our own four children range in age from thirty-five to forty-one years, I hope that one or more of our grandchildren will take advantage of these weekends and any of the other wonderful academic opportunities offered by Duke TIP!

Academic Adventures, one-day programs for students who have participated in the fourth- and fifth-grade talent search, provide hands-on, experiential learning opportunities.

Independent Learning is for students who cannot necessarily access campus-based sites; Duke TIP CD-ROM provides courses for motivated and self-directed gifted students and an opportunity to explore subjects of personal interest, guided by an expert mentor.

Other educational resources and initiatives include:

- *The Duke Gifted Letter*, a quarterly newsletter for the parents of gifted and talented children;
- *The Duke TIP Family Conference*, held annually in conjunction with Duke TIP's Grand Recognition Ceremony;
- *Advanced Placement Manuals and Workshops*; and
- *Research* provide benefits to gifted children and their parents, including original research conducted by Duke TIP staff;
- *The Next Generation Venture Fund*, a partnership among Duke TIP, the Goldman Sachs Foundation, the John Hopkins Center for Talented Youth, and other entities, invests in talented young people from underrepresented groups who have the potential to succeed in the classroom, in college, and in demanding professions.

I can't support Duke TIP enough for all the current and future opportunities it is and will provide for today's gifted youth and their parents.

39

MEADOW

Rosemary Callard-Szulgit

Dr. Luanne Burns developed a procedural diagnostic tool, MEADOW (Mathematics, Errors and Automatic Debugging of Written input), as part of her dissertation study at Columbia University in 1993. The domain of the tool and the study was children's subtraction. MEADOW incorporates the content and sequence of handwritten marks made during the execution of a mathematics procedure into the knowledge base of an expert system.

Dr. Burns was able to show that explanatory feedback is clearly more effective than error signaling. She also clarified that both domain-based and student-based feedback yield strong outcomes and do not appear to differ significantly.

As educators, we anxiously await Dr. Burns' MEADOW on the market as one more valuable tool to help us provide math excellence in our classrooms.

40

MOSS MEADOW SCHOOL

Rosemary Callard-Szulgit

A school I had the privilege of visiting in the private sector of education is the Moss Meadow School (Shillelagh Road, Chesapeake, VA 23323, mossmeadowschool@aol.com). Its founders, Dr. Gary Moss and Suzanne Rubin Moss, are true visionaries.

Moss Meadow School is located on a beautiful seven-acre property in sunny Chesapeake, VA. It is a school where childhood is honored and the freedom to learn, develop, and pursue individual interest and talents is encouraged and supported.

Mornings for these sixty-five students, ages four to seventeen, begin with a community meeting, providing time to reflect individually and collectively. Following this meeting, children ages four to six go to the Nature Room, where fairy-tale hideaways inspire children's imaginations and creativity. High-quality learning materials provide the experiential-based foundation for academic learning that is vital to young children.

Individual students are given the opportunity to learn independently in six classrooms upstairs in this lovely country home. Each student works with a curriculum that has been chosen specifically for him or her and each works at his or her own pace. Mentors are available in each classroom to assist as needed and keep the continuity of integrated learning and independent academic goals supported. As I visited the math and science rooms with all their laboratory equipment, computers, books, and support materials, I couldn't help but visualize a future Nobel Prize winner!

When the formal study time of the morning ends, students are free to choose how they will spend the remainder of the day. Again, mentors are available to inspire and assist the children as needed. In the afternoon at Moss Meadow, the focus is not on learning in the traditional sense, but by giving children the time and space to enjoy being children. This is such a vital part of the school day. Creativity can blossom as children peacefully relax either indoors or outdoors, letting their brains incubate on the day's earlier learning or any other ideas and discussions from previous experiences.

Each day concludes with a meeting in which all members of the school community share their day's experiences.

41

THE NORTH CAROLINA SCHOOL OF SCIENCE AND MATHEMATICS

Rosemary Callard-Szulgit

Just before completing my part of the writing for this book, I had the pleasure of spending a morning at the North Carolina School of Science and Mathematics (NCSSM), a wonderful public, residential, coeducational high school for juniors and seniors with high intellectual ability and commitment to scholarship. I started my visit with an introduction to Dr. Steve Warshaw, senior vice-president for academic affairs, who would meet me later for an interview and graciously answer my multitude of questions. I then went on a tour with Jeanne Chen, a junior at the school. We never stopped talking! I was so excited to be on a campus where respect for learning was apparent and professional courtesies abounded.

I started by asking Jeanne what the major difference was between her former high school and NCSSM. She immediately replied, "In my home high school, I already knew most of the work. Here, I am challenged every day! We each strive for our own personal excellence."

Jeanne's reply pretty much summed up my entire experience at NCSSM that morning. Everywhere we went, I saw students dedicated to learning—mature, happy young adults, socially interactive with each other and with any other adults in their proximity.

In the music conservatory, I met Mr. Laird, who was just getting a rehearsal started for the school's spring concert of Haydn's *Mass in D Minor*. I also visited the recording studio, where students are taught about and experience professional recordings. The art studio and classrooms were next, with the beautiful stained-glass windows designed and made by former students.

It was obvious that the faculty members were talented, well trained, and committed to their fields of expertise and to the students at NCSSM. Counseling and support services were plentiful. It would be hard for kids to fail here. There is an overriding commitment to excellence and success for everyone.

Dr. Warshaw proudly pointed out the school's Distance Learning Program, an information highway for cyber campuses. Coupled with a trimester calendar, the school's philosophy is to ensure that each student obtains a thorough grounding in the sciences, mathematics, language arts, history, and a foreign language; that each becomes proficient in the use of computers, laboratory facilities, and other means by which knowledge is acquired and processed in the sciences and mathematics; and that each adopts a sequence of study that includes investigating areas of academic interest in depth through high-level course offerings and such activities as mentorship, research courses, independent studies, seminars, directed group studies and mini-term.

I applaud the North Carolina School of Science and Mathematics as one more opportunity open to all of North Carolina's bright students with specific interests and talents to study, accelerate, learn, laugh, honor, and grow as young adults. Contact them at NCSSM, 1219 Broad Street, Durham, NC 27705, www.ncssm.edu.

VI

REFLECTIONS ON EDUCATION

DID YOU KNOW YOU'RE MY HERO?

Rosemary Callard-Szulgit, Kristina Kirchgraber, Barbara Messmer, Tige Noni, and Michael Bittlingmaier

During one of our class discussions this past semester, I was once again emphasizing the importance of an exceptional teacher in the classroom. School districts can budget "all the money in the world," seeking a fine education for their children—but it's the teachers who can make or break our children.

It suddenly dawned on me! I should have my graduate students write about their education heroes/heroines, sharing these grand and noble educators with others. I also asked my students to remember a painful experience with an educator, to get it out and forgive the teacher. I found it amazing to hear some of the stories and how many years and decades some of these students had carried this pain. Hopefully, forgiveness has occurred and their spirits are freer.

My friend and second-grade colleague Colleen is an inspiration to me. She is someone who makes "my heart full" and takes my breath away as a teacher and as a person. She has a love for her profession like no one I've ever seen. Whereas most people dread the students that come into their classroom as low readers and writers, Colleen rises to the challenge. She focuses all her energy into getting those kids to like reading and writing with as much love as if they were her own children. Conversations with her very rarely consist of anything outside of reading and writing strategies, success stories with her students in those areas, and searches for ways to expand (reading and writing) programs. Equally important to her is balancing her curriculum to include those students who need enrichment. She has inspired me to look at each child as an individual student and to gear his or her needs accordingly. More importantly, she has allowed me to think outside the "typical education box" and to let students take responsibility for their education by supplying differentiated choices for them. She is a true teacher dedicated to her students' success in life.

by Kristina Kirchgraber
Second Grade, Brockport, NY

One person who has strengthened me as a person and as a student is one of my former students. He was a great kid with terrific math abilities that were not coming out because of a language problem. He had difficulty making connections. When I worked with him I told him math had rules like Monopoly. In Monopoly, you get $200 every time you pass "Go." In math, you follow the "Order of Operations" and always do parentheses first, then exponents, multiply or divide, and lastly add or subtract. Math had rules just like the game.

We also improved his writing and analytical skills by connecting situations to things he liked to do, such as belonging to Boy Scouts and camping. We would use what he knew from his experiences outside the classroom to connect to class work. No one had ever done this type of thing before with him. They didn't teach him that working on his geology badge in Boy Scouts could help him with his Earth Science. No one ever showed him they were parts of the same subject.

He has graduated from our school and gone on to high school. Any time I see him, I know he made a difference in my life and I made a difference in his life.

Thanks so much for thinking of me,
Barbara Messmer

In my undergraduate career (before knowing that I wanted to teach), I had a professor who opened my eyes. His name is Dr. Richard Mancuso, and he teaches physics at the State University of New York at

Brockport. I was required to take physics, but did not want to, because I thought it was going to be hard. These fears also manifested from preconceived notions that I had about physics. The thoughts also (probably) came from having former teachers hint to the idea that I was an average or below average student.

The first day of physics class was a nightmare. Dr. Mancuso made us sit in the front two rows and he struck the fear of God in everyone with his expectations. I plugged along with the course and continued struggling (along with everyone else). By the middle of the first semester (I had to take two semesters of physics, back to back), I started enjoying the course and the challenge. Dr. Mancuso made the class fun and challenging. By not giving direct answers to us, we had to search out the answers by ourselves. Each new problem and solution boosted the confidence of everyone in class.

Long story short, Dr. Mancuso tore away misconceptions that I had for decades, misconceptions that I had about physics as well as about myself. He is one of the great teachers I have had and one of the reasons I am teaching today.

Thanks, Dr. M.

Sincerely,
Tige Noni

My greatest teacher was my brother. Four years older than I, he always seemed to be on top of things in a place I could never reach. He was handsome, athletic, smart, and sprayed with Teflon (never got into trouble). The first twenty years of my life, he was my hero. However, the next ten, I resented him for his gifts and arrogance. I always got caught doing the wrong things while he never did . . . until his first trouble with the law would put him in jail for eight years (drug trafficking.) For eight years I watched him broken and humbled behind bars. When he came out (two years ago), he embraced all the things that are important, including family, integrity, and hard work. We're best friends now and he's my hero again. I have learned that people have an incredible ability to change for the better, no matter how unchangeable they may seem. I try to look at my students every day and think about their limitless possibilities. I will never pigeonhole a child and assess whether he or she "has it" or not. All children have it. They just have to find it and as their teacher, I can help.

by Michael Bittlingmaier

43

I FORGIVE YOU

Brenda Mashiotta, Megann Perrotti,
Tracy Farnand, and Kristina Kirchgraber

In the fourth grade, I had a teacher named Mrs. Brown. I looked forward to learning in school and loved to learn but I'll admit I was quite the social butterfly in school. I looked forward to seeing my friends every day. Being the tomboy I was, I also looked forward to recess more than anything. I probably did not try my best at school at this time of my educational experience.

However, I remember the first time I was allowed to write a paper about my own topic—I *LOVED* it!

I did not usually enjoy being told what to do—especially when it came to writing. We *always* had to write about a given topic and never allowed the freedom of free write in Mrs. Brown's class until this day.

So, I wrote my paper pouring my whole heart into it (something I normally did not do on the specific topic papers)! I received a "Do Over" on the paper because Mrs. Brown said it was definitely not MY work; that my mother or my sister must have written it for me.

Yikes!!

Broke my heart.

Dear Mrs. Brown,

You, fortunately, were my only negative memory of school . . . but you lit a fire under me and to this day I always do my BEST in ALL I do!
—Brenda Mashiotta

In third grade, we had to write a story about our family. I wrote a story about my father, dog, and myself that I thought was pretty good. A few days later, the teacher had graded the papers. She wrote a sentence on the board that said, "Me and my dad took the dog for a walk." She then told everyone it was a sentence from my paper and corrected it, making it seem like it should have been so obvious that it should have been "My dad and I." I was so embarrassed in front of the whole class and concentrated way more on grammar and mechanics than creativity after that.

Dear Mrs. Real,

It really embarrassed me when you showed the whole class my mistake. *You didn't have to tell them whose it was.* To this day, I am fanatical about grammar. Please don't embarrass students like that. It makes them not want to share anything.

Sincerely,
Megann Perrotti

When I was in first grade, I had a teacher who was very unfair. She favored the boys over the girls and always sided with them. While most of the boys carried an A throughout the year, the girls barely got by with a C. If we were really lucky she would provide us with a C + ! One certain time, I remember that she stifled my creativity was when we were working on a project. It was a child's favorite assignment: use scissors, paper, glue, and crayons and do whatever you want to make a collage. I was ecstatic! I loved to be creative! I worked very hard on my project and when I was almost finished, I noticed the boy who sat next to me hadn't even started. While I was finishing up, I noticed him watching me and doing what I did. I didn't say anything to the teacher because she would have made me be quiet and sit with my head down for tattling. The next day when she was passing back the projects, I didn't receive mine. When I asked her about it, she said that mine looked just like Ricky's, and that since it was obvious that *I* copied *him*, I would have to stay inside for recess and do mine again. I was devastated and I tried to explain that he copied me, but she wouldn't listen and told me to go sit down and behave. To this day, I am always a little apprehensive about doing creative projects. First grade was such a tough grade for me, and having a teacher like her didn't help!

Letter to my teacher:
Dear Mrs. Hucknall,

I am writing this letter to tell you that even though you made first grade really hard for me, I have now finally been able to put it behind me. When we were doing our creative projects, I never really felt like I could do creative things because you stifled that in me. You were very unfair to the girls and it made me really upset. I have gone on to become a teacher and I will never treat my students with the unfairness that you showed! I have been able to work past the treatment that I received in your class because I had a lot of wonderful teachers. Because of them, I have been able to forgive you, but I will never forget the hurt and embarrassment that you caused me in first grade!

Sincerely,
Tracy Farnand

I went to a Catholic school for my thirteen years of education. There was no differentiation or modifications, nor was there room for errors. My teachers for the most part were nuns and priests. Then one year, in fifth grade, they hired a man (in his thirties) to be our teacher. He was not a priest. He was fun, caring, open to new ideas, enjoyed learning, encouraged us as learners, and above all, he knew and accepted our differences academically. School was now an enjoyable place to be and not some place where we were all robots. Every day was a new adventure. He taught outside the box and let us learn at our levels. We all loved him. However, he was not loved by the other staff members. By the end of the year, he was gone and the following school year started with a new fifth-grade teacher—a priest—and the beat goes on! School after then was boring and mundane—something we had to get through.

Dear Diocese of Buffalo,

I wish to express my thanks to you for taking away the one bright light in my young educational career. Thank you for giving me the strength to become someone that I admired that was taken away for thinking outside the teaching box. Because of your decision, I have learned what drives students to love school and have successfully become that person. So you see, you cannot stifle growth and change no matter how hard you try.

Thank you.

Kristina Kirchgraber
Second Grade Teacher, Brockport, NY

GIFTED CHILDREN SPEAK TO US

Rosemary Callard-Szulgit

Every summer for over twenty years I ran a two-week cultural arts institute for gifted nine- to thirteen-year-olds. On the very last morning, I would take a peaceful hour with them—soft lights, easy music—and tell the story of Kahlil Gibran's *The Prophet*. I would then ask the children to honor me by being my prophet, answering some of the age-old questions of humankind.

So many readers have commented on their delight in reading my gifted students' responses in my three former books that I've added many new quips and kept some of my favorites for you here.

Enjoy.

SPEAK TO ME ABOUT CHILDREN

- Great, fun, neat, cool, awesome, smart. (Shifra, age 10)
- Sometimes they can be annoying and hard to understand and sometimes nice and easy to understand. (Mandy, age 9)
- Children are brats when young, independent when old, and sometimes carry over into adulthood. (Jeff, age 11)
- They fill their parents up with love and joy. (Karen, age 9)
- Children are like the seed of the future to me. They are the people who will change the world tomorrow and will succeed in doing so. They are different from adults in a way that they stretch their hands

out to the stars and try new things. They are free at heart, mind, and spirit. (Shelly, age 9)

SPEAK TO ME ABOUT SCHOOL

- Some teachers let you learn and then others tell you to do exactly as you are told and if you go beyond what they want, you are in big trouble. (Bryan, age 10)
- School is a place where learning is the key and being with friends is an especially fun part. (Aileen, age 9)
- Hard, scary, frustrating, enjoyable. (Sara, age 9)
- Boring lots, fun sometimes, hate textbooks because it would be funner to be creative learning. (Mandy, age 9)
- School is long and tedious. It doesn't allow you much free time. (Jeff, age 11)
- School is a place where average students learn. Gifted students learn anywhere else. (Carl, age 11)

SPEAK TO ME ABOUT TEACHERS

- They're too mean. (Chris, age 10)
- You can always find something nice in each one. (Mandy, age 9)
- Teachers are some of the people that bring knowledge to all children. (Joe, age 9)
- Curious, interesting, happy, helpful, scary. (Sara, age 9)
- Once in a while you'll cross paths with great teachers who put their mark on you forever. (Leila, age 9)
- Teachers are anyone and everyone who have a lesson to teach or tale to tell. (Shannon, age 10)

SPEAK TO ME ABOUT PARENTS

- They're great, they buy everything for you. (Chris, age 10)
- Nice almost at all times. I hate it when they're mad. (Mandy, age 9)

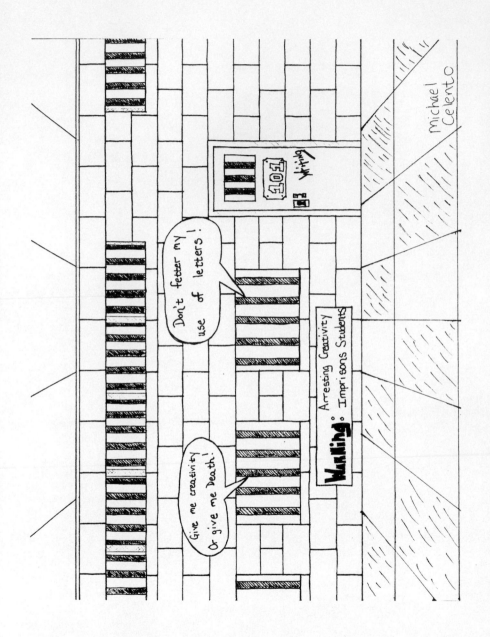

Julie
Knapp

- Parents don't understand. They are unfair and too protective. (Jeff, age 11)
- Parents are people who shine light on the path of life, even though they cannot walk the whole journey with their children. (Carl, age 11)
- Parents are the gatekeepers of the "younger generation." (Shannon, age 10)

SPEAK TO ME ABOUT LOVE

- Love is the caring and support people give each other. Some people even say that love is what makes the world go around. (Karen, age 9)
- Love is caring, kindness and thoughtfulness to anyone near or dear to someone's heart. (Shannon, age 10)

SPEAK TO ME ABOUT WHAT IS IMPORTANT TO YOU

- Getting more friends. (Bryan, age 10)
- My computer. (Chris age 10)
- Love. (Shifra, age 10)
- Always trying my hardest at everything and being nice to everyone. (Mandy, age 9)
- That my parents like me. (Trevor, age 9)
- Everything that I have said is important to me. (Joe, age 9)

A LETTER TO PARENTS

Sarah Groom

Mom, Dad, there is something that I do not understand:

I do not understand why so many of the other students in my class receive the support they need in order to increase their knowledge, while I am patiently listening to my teacher tell me information and ideas that I already know! Aren't teachers concerned that I also expand my mind?

Try to imagine what it would be like to be in this position. How much fun would it be to listen to someone explain information that you already know? Yes, individuals can definitely learn more about all topics by studying subject material in a deeper manner. However, I cannot imagine that the overwhelming majority of teachers are going out of their way to take gifted students to deeper levels. Yes, I do see teachers providing extra work for such students. Is extra work the solution that teachers choose to help students with special needs to improve? No. Students with special needs receive much time, attention, and thought from their teachers. Just as it is not right to give all attention to the "average students," it is not right to give all attention to the "lower" students.

Our school days begin with Sam, Joey, Karen, and Andy leaving the classroom to work with Mrs. Resource while the rest of us have guided reading time. I don't know exactly what these classmates do with Mrs. Resource. Could they be having more fun than me? Do they too have to sit in desks or in circles, reading easy books, only to then answer basic

comprehension questions on the material read? On the bus, I heard
some girls in AP English talking about some synthesis projects that they
are working on in response to Nathaniel Hawthorne's Scarlet Letter.
How I wish I could read books like that in school and then apply my
mind to what I read!

Again, we as teachers try to give students with special needs what
they need in order to succeed, but are we giving gifted students the
material and time they also deserve in order to reach their potential?

We should strive to bring all students to the "synthesis" level of
thought through our teaching. When teachers focus on the lower levels
of thought, students do not really learn information—basic recall questions do not require much thought and other answers may be easily
memorized and forgotten.

Once reading time ends, Mrs. Push-In joins us to monitor Dan and Sal-
ly's progress as we work on our writing. During this time, my frustra-
tion continues to build because Mrs. Tradition, my general education
teacher, likes to give us assigned topics to write about—I don't want to
write about what I did over the weekend. I want to write about more
important things; I want to have a purpose for writing—I think I might
like to write a letter to the president asking him what he is planning on
doing to alleviate the problems we are having in our country. Actually,
I am writing this letter to you just because my teachers are standing
over my shoulder and telling me that I have to write a friendly letter!

The frustration expressed in this paragraph is not unique to gifted
students. Giving the students ownership over their work is good child-
centered teaching philosophy in practice. Often gifted students think
about big problems in the world.

Mrs. Push-In stays in our room during math time and provides basic
definitions and extra support for all of the previously mentioned class-
mates. I wish she would pay more attention to me because I don't always
understand what we are learning. I can read the textbook just fine, but
honestly, I don't understand how we are supposed to use all of the num-
bers. Why do I have to learn math anyway? I don't really want Mrs.

Push-In to know I am struggling in math because I am excelling in everything else. I would feel like a failure if other people really knew how difficult math is for me. One day, I overheard Mrs. Push-In talking to Mrs. Tradition. Mrs. Tradition named specific students that Mrs. Push-In should focus on helping. When my name appeared on the list, Mrs. Push-In inquired about it. Mrs. Tradition replied that I am only on the list because I am not working hard enough in math. She said that if I am "so gifted" I should be above the classmates in all areas of my work, so I must be slacking off. Because she feels this way, I am left on my own to learn.

Many gifted students are perfectionists. Perfectionists do not like to fail in anything. Not all gifted students are "gifted across the board." At this point, you should have an image of a gifted student who excels in English language arts and struggles in math. How would you feel to have everyone continually expect great things from you, but to fall short in one area? I am sure that this student would be hard enough on himself or herself without the help of teachers showing their disapproval.

After lunch, the rest of the day is a blur. Don't get me wrong, it is not that we are moving at a faster pace through material—I have just basically had it with being patient and attentive, so I entertain myself. During this time, I usually think about one topic after another, or I try to quickly finish my class work in order to continue reading another book of my choice.

If you were in the place of this student, how long would you politely sit at your desk and be content with boredom?

Mom and Dad, I don't know what to do. I need someone to speak up for me. Can you help?

—Sarah Groom

Adrienne Ripley

THREE POPULAR QUESTIONS AND COMMONSENSE ANSWERS ABOUT GIFTED CHILDREN AND THEIR EDUCATION

Rosemary Callard-Szulgit

Q. (Teacher) I recently graded one of my high school student's writing assignments (a movie review) with a B. The student in question, Missy, had an absolute fit, saying she had done her best and wanted to know what rubric I had used to grade the assignment! To say she was irate for not earning an A is an understatement! Do you have any suggestions to deal with a situation such as this?

A. Yes. While a rubric is a valuable assessment tool, not all assignments can be graded so systematically. I believe we have gone overboard with rubric grading and need to leave room for affective grading and assessments. You more than likely graded this piece based on originality and insightfulness of thought. An A or A+ response would have been a truly striking paper, intellectually and emotionally. Apparently Missy's response was not exceptional from your point of view, but was very good. It sounds to me like Missy has issues with perfectionism and would be wise to seek help from you or a counselor. Meanwhile, if this happens again with a student, use my response above and suggest the student takes a few days to reflect. If he or she is still irate, then come back and speak again with you . . . speak, not attack!

Q. (Parent) My husband and I are hearing so much about attention deficit hyperactivity disorder (ADHD) and Asperger's syndrome. It

seems to be a large focus of teacher and parent dialogue now. Can you
provide some clarity for us, please?

A. Of course.

ADHD is a recognized and very treatable condition with stimulant
medications in 3–5 percent of children. Its subtypes include predomi-
nantly hyperactive and predominately inattentive. Combined brain cir-
cuitry involving a part of the prefrontal cortex, and the basal ganglia
seem to be affected in children diagnosed with ADHD; the structures
can be smaller and less active, and their use of dopamine is altered.
Scientists are now linking genetic heritability with ADHD to a very
large extent.

I remember vividly the inclusion classroom I had once with thirty-
three students tripping over each other and me, twelve of whom were
identified as ADHD, and three of whom were not yet receiving any
medications. It was that year I learned to completely understand the
phrase "baptism under fire!" The classroom was an impossible learning
situation for all of us. I always greeted every student at the door and
either shook or held his or her hand with a personal verbal welcome.
When Jennie was twenty feet away, I could already tell she had forgotten her medicine! One of the boys, Brad, went on a three-week trial in
which he, his parents, and I would rate his behaviors, focus, and so on,
without any of us knowing whether his pills were a placebo or the real
thing. There was a marked and clear difference during the week. Brad
was on the appropriate medication.

I know it can be a heartbreaking decision for parents to seek appropriate medication for a child who has been diagnosed with ADHD, especially with all the press concerning overdiagnosis. However, I
encourage any parent to have his or her child participate in the clinical
three-week trials if she or he is suspected as a candidate with ADHD.
The results, I'm sure, will bring peace and understanding to your decision for diagnosis and possible treatment. Research continues to support the effective and positive use of medication alone and/or
medication with psychological behavioral treatments combined as a way
to help and support children with ADHD.

Coupled with myths surrounding gifted children, there also seems to
be growing confusion about gifted children with Asperger's and "twice
exceptional children." Little (2002) helps clear up some of the common

misunderstandings and confusion between gifted traits and Asperger's syndrome traits in the following table:

Asperger's	Gifted	Twice Exceptional
• Advanced vocabulary	• Advanced vocabulary	• Advanced vocabulary
• Unaware of another's perspective	• Ability to see another's viewpoint	• Unaware of another's perspective
• Literal thought	• High abstract thinking skills	• Intensity of focus
• Poor language comprehension	• Good language comprehension	• Sensory sensitivity
• Intensity of focus	• Intensity of focus	• Introverted
• Introverted	• Introverted	• Enjoys "rote" exercises
• Excellent memory	• Excellent memory	• Poor language comprehension
• Sensory sensitivity	• Sensitivity toward others	

The author does note that there are many commonalities between the lists and the reader should note what motivation is behind each behavior.

Kirby describes Asperger's syndrome as follows:

Asperger Syndrome or (Asperger's Disorder) is a neurobiological disorder named for a Viennese physician, Hans Asperger, who in 1944 published a paper which described a pattern of behaviors in several young boys who had normal intelligence and language development, but who also exhibited autistic-like behaviors and marked deficiencies in social and communication skills. In spite of the publication of his paper in the 1940s, it wasn't until 1994 that Asperger Syndrome was added to the DSM IV and only in the past few years has AS been recognized by professionals and parents.

Individuals with AS can exhibit a variety of characteristics and the disorder can range from mild to severe. Persons with AS show marked deficiencies in social skills, have difficulties with transitions or changes and prefer sameness. They often have obsessive routines and may be preoccupied with a particular subject of interest. They have a great deal of difficulty reading nonverbal cues (body language) and very often the individual with AS has difficulty determining proper body space. Often overly sensitive to sounds, tastes, smells, and sights, the person with AS may prefer soft clothing, certain foods, and be bothered by sounds or lights no one else seems to hear or see. It's important to remember that the person with AS perceives the world very differently. Therefore, many

behaviors that seem odd or unusual are due to those neurological differences and not the result of intentional rudeness or bad behavior, and most
certainly not the result of 'improper parenting.'(2005)

> http://www.udel.edu/bkirby/asperger/aswhatisit.html
> accessed 2005

I feel it is crucial to clear up some of the misunderstandings surrounding gifted and Asperger's, as many educators currently seem to be
doing. One of my friends has a wonderfully gifted four-year-old son who
is currently being treated for Asperger's. What I find appalling is that
Julia was told by her son's psychologist that 80 percent of gifted children
have Asperger's. I was so enraged when I heard that statistic quoted that
I asked for the documentation and research to validate that statement.
Neither I nor Julia has received copies of such research and I have encouraged Julia to find a different psychologist!

If you review Little's list, you'll note a distinction between a child
with an advanced vocabulary who is unaware of another's perspective
and a child with an advanced vocabulary and the ability to see another's
viewpoint! Literal thought is certainly different than high abstract thinking skills.

It's been my experience throughout my career in gifted education
that the majority of gifted kids I've worked with are far more extro-
verted than introverted, so I need to challenge that item on Little's list.

Q.   (Student) As a college student, I can see the definite advantages of
my classmates who have had or currently have mentors in their lives. In
fact, I would like to give this gift to other children and adults. I have
quite an expertise in photography and would love to help aspiring camera buffs.

Can you help me both find a mentor for myself in cinematography
and also connect with students who would benefit from my learning?
A.   I know exactly how you feel. Having grown up in a small town and
having attended a SUNY college, I never had the luxury of an academic
mentor. I was pretty much a product of the standard teacher/lecture/
memorize/get As/then forget most of the information included on the
tests after they were over. Thank goodness times are changing and we're

realizing all children should be taken to the synthesis level, which provides creativity and thinking for all.

You can make a difference as a mentor and I'm happy to help. Here are some popular programs for you to access on the Internet:

UConn Mentor Connection (www.gifted.uconn.edu/mentoruc
.html)

Mentoring Partnership (www.mentoring.org)

IMentor (www.imentor.org)

Mentoring Group (www.mentoringgroup.com)

Best wishes to you!

APPENDIX A: AWARDS

THE NATIONAL INSTITUTES OF HEALTH

The National Institutes of Health are funding science education partnership grants, designed to help scientists work with educators and local
organizations to boost K–12 students' understanding of science and
health. Deadline is October 1. Grants can be of any size less than
$300,000. For more information, contact National Institutes of Health,
Paul Karadbil, at (301) 435-0844, or e-mail: paulk@ncrr.nih.gov.

LOWE'S

The Lowe's Charitable and Educational Foundation funds small-scale
projects near their stores. The foundation considers any type of education based on community needs and store managers' expertise. Funding
levels vary depending on your school's proposal. Managers accept applications anytime. For more information, contact Lowe's Foundation,
David Loiver, at (333) 658-4000, or use your favorite search engine with
the keywords "Lowe's community involvement." Alternatively, you can
go to: http://www.lowes.com/lowes/lkn?action = pg&p = AboutLowes/
Community

APPENDIX B: CENTERS FOR GIFTED EDUCATION AND TALENT SEARCHES

Belin-Blank International Center for Gifted Education and Talent Development (BESTS)
> Talent searches grades 2–9; commuter and residential programs grades 3–12.
> The University of Iowa, Iowa City, IA
> www.education.uiowa.edu/belinblank

Carnegie Mellon Institute for Talented Elementary Students (C-MITES)
> Talent search, grades 3–6; commuter programs throughout Pennsylvania, grades K–7.
> Carnegie Mellon University, Pittsburgh, PA
> www.cmu.edu/cmites

Center for Talent Development (CTD)
> The LearningLinks Program (formerly LetterLinks) is designed for independent learning and offers students in sixth through twelfth grades honors-level and Advanced Placement courses for high school credit. Northwestern University provides this program. The website lists other distance learning opportunities.
> www.ctd.northwestern.edu

Center for Talented Youth (CTY)
> Commuter and residential programs, elementary and secondary students; correspondence courses for various ages.

Johns Hopkins University, Baltimore, MD
www.cty.jhu.edu

Davidson Institute for Talent Development
To recognize, nurture, and support profoundly intelligent young
people.
Reno, NV
www.ditd.org

Education Program for Gifted Youth (EPGY)
This program provided by Stanford University offers accelerated
course work for gifted students from kindergarten through high
school. Presently, more than 3,000 students from around the world
are enrolled in EPGY program.
www.epgy.Stanford.edu/overview/infor.html

Frances A. Karnes Center for Gifted Studies
Grades 7–10
The University of Southern Mississippi, Hattiesburg, MS
www.dept.usm.edu/~gifted

The Gelfand Outreach Program in Mathematics (GOPM)
Rutgers University Center for Mathematics, Science, and Computer
Education provides this program for middle and high school students. Students work at their own pace and enjoy the benefit of individual feedback from a GOPM mentor who reads all of their work
and provides individual responses. For further information call (732)
445–3491 or e-mail gopm@math.rutgers.edu.

Hampshire College Summer Studies in Mathematics
Programs for mathematically talented and motivated high school students.
Hampshire College, Amherst, MA
www.hcssim.org

The Internet Academy
The Internet Academy provides courses and teachers to students via
the Internet. Washington State certified teachers provide instruction

to students in grades K–12. The program allows for innovative uses of technology, customized learning environments, and access to skilled instructors.
www.iacademy.org/IA/AboutUs/Welcome.html

Program in Mathematics for Young Scientists (PROMYS)
A challenging program designed to encourage ambitious high school students to explore the creative world of mathematics.
Boston University, Boston, MA
http://math.bu.edu/people/promys

Purdue University of Gifted Education Resource Institute
Grades 7–12
Purdue University, West Lafayette, IN
www.geri.soe.purdue.edu

Research Science Institute
A mentor program in the sciences for rising high school seniors.
Vienna, VA
www.cee.org/rsi/

Ross Mathematics Program
For fourteen- to seventeen-year-olds deeply interested in math and science. Intense math courses.
Ohio State University, Columbus, OH
www.math.ohio-state.edu/ross

Summer Program for Verbally and Mathematically Precocious Youth
Grades 7–10
The Center for Gifted Studies
Western Kentucky University, Bowling Green, KY
www.wku.edu/gifted

Talented Identification Program (TIP)
Residential summer program for grades 7–12. Educational information provided to grades 4–6.
Duke University, Durham, NC
www.tip.duke.edu

University of Minnesota Talented Youth Mathematics Program (UM-TYMP)
> Commuter program in accelerated mathematics for students in grades 5–12. Institute of Technology Center for Educational Programs.
> University of Minnesota, Minneapolis, MN
> www.math.umn.edu/itcep/umtymp

Virtual School for the Gifted (VSG)
> The VSG is an online school that specializes in providing enrichment courses to complement and extend the regular curriculum. The VSG works with schools and home schools to provide courses to challenge able students.
> www.vsg.edu.au

APPENDIX C:
MATH AND SCIENCE BOOKS

I asked teachers, parents, and students to submit lists of some of their favorite math and science books. From that list, I selected a variety of authors and styles that, I hope, will be especially helpful to your children and young adults. The age categories are very general and should be taken with a grain of salt. Check each book to ensure that it is appropriate for your child or young adult before purchasing a copy. Because young adults are usually reading textbooks for math and science, we focused on fiction and other "ancillary" reading for that section.

ELEMENTARY BOOKS

Author	Title	Copyright	Publisher
Albee, Sarah	*The Oreo Cookie Counting Book*	2000	Simon & Schuster
Allen, Judy	*Are You a Butterfly?*	2000	Kingfisher
Mitsumasa Anno	*Anno's Counting Book*	1975	HarperCollins
Anno, Masiachiro, and Anno, Mitsumasa	*Anno's Mysterious Multiplying Jar*	1983	Philomel Books
Anonymous	*Go Ask Alice*	1971	Simon and Schuster
Applegate, Katherine	*Aftermath*	2003	Scholastic
Applegate, Katherine	*Dream Storm*	2003	Scholastic
Arnold, Nick	*Ugly Bug*	1999	Scholastic
Axelrod, Amy	*Pigs Will Be Pigs*	1994	Aladdin Paperbacks

Banks, Lynne Reid	*The Indian in the Cupboard*	1999	HarperTrophy
Barnes, Kate and Steve Weston	*How It Works: The Human Body*	1995	Backpack
Barrett, Judi	*Cloudy with a Chance of Meatballs*	1978	Scholastic
Barrett, Judi	*Pickles to Pittsburgh*	1997	Scholastic
Brandenberg, Aliki	*My Five Senses*	1989	Ty Crowell, Co.
Brown, Jeff	*Stanley In Space*	1990	Scholastic
Brown, Margaret Wise	*The Important Book*	1949	Harper & Row
Burke, Rick	*Benjamin Banneker*	1978	Abingdon Press
Burns, Marilyn	*Spaghetti and Meatballs For All: A Mathematical Story*	1997	Scholastic
Burns, Marilyn	*The Greedy Triangle*	1994	Scholastic
Carle, Eric	*A House for Hermit Crab*	1987	Picture Book Studio
Carle, Eric	*The Tiny Seed*	1987	Picture Book Studio
Carle, Eric	*The Very Hungry Caterpillar*	1983	Philomel
Casey, Denise	*Weather Everywhere*	1995	Macmillan
Cherry, Lynne	*The Great Kapok Tree*	1994	Philomel
Cole, Joanna	*The Magic School Bus Series*	1995	Scholastic
Crews, Donald	*Freight Train*	1996	Greenwillow, Board
Daniels, Teri	*Math Man*	2001	Scholastic
D'Andrea, Debbie	*Reese's Pieces Math Fun 1 to 9*	2001	Nimble Me
DeLuise, Dom	*Charlie the Caterpillar*	1990	Aladdin Paperbacks
de Paola, Tomi	*The Popcorn Book*	1984	Holiday House
Durham, Meredith	*Numbers How Do You Say It?*	1987	Lothrop Lee & Shep.
Elhert, Lois	*Red Leaf, Yellow Leaf*	1991	Harcourt Brace
Gibbons, Gail	*Weather Words and What They Mean*	1990	Scholastic
Goldish, Meish	*101 Science Poems & Songs for Young Learners*	1996	Scholastic
Graham, Ian, Barbara Taylor, John Frandon, and Chris Oxdale	*Science Encyclopedia*	1999	Paragon
Gundersen, P. Erik	*The Handy Physics Answer Book*	1999	Visible Ink Press
Hiaasen, Carl	*Hoot*	2002	Alfred A. Knofp
Hutchins, Pat	*Clocks and More Clocks*	1970	Scholastic

Johnson, Jay	What's Inside the Magic Box? Using Personal Computers in the 21st Century	1991	Gifted Education
Kent, Jack	The Caterpillar and the Polliwog	1982	Aladdin Paperbacks
King, Elizabeth	The Pumpkin Patch	1990	E.P. Dutton
Kunhardt, Edith I.	Pompeii Buried Alive	1987	Sagebrush Education
Levine, Shar	First Science Experiments	2004	Sterling
Lord, Bette Bao	In the Year of the Boar and Jackie Robinson	1984	Harper Trophy
Lowry, Lois	Gathering Blue	2002	Laurel Leaf
Lowry, Lois	The Giver	2000	Laurel Leaf
Mathews, Louise	Gator Pie	1979	Dodd, Mead & Co.
McGrath, Barbara	The M&M's Counting Book	1994	Charlesbridge
Mellett, Peter	Trees	2000	Sagebrush Ed. Res.
Middleton, Haydn	Thomas Edison	2001	Ipicturebooks
Morris, Richard	Cosmic Questions	1993	John Wiley & Sons
Myller, Rolf	How Big Is a Foot?	1986	Penguin
Murphy, Stuart	Give Me Half!	1996	HarperCollins
Neuschwander, Cindy	Sir Cumference and the First Round Table: A Math Adventure	1997	Charlesbridge
O'Dell, Scott	Island of the Blue Dolphins	1960	Houghton Mifflin
Pallotta, Jerry	The Hershey's Book Series	2000	Scholastic
Pallotta, Jerry	Hershey's Weights and Measures	2002	Scholastic
Pearon, Donna	Math4Today	1997	Good Apple
Pinczes, Elinor J.	A Remainder of One	1995	Houghton Mifflin
Pinczes, Elinor J.	One Hundred Hungry Ants	1982	Houghton Mifflin
Reimer, Luetta	Mathematicians Are People Too: Stories from the Lives of Great Mathematicians	1990	Pearson Learning
Robinson, Fay	Fantastic Frogs	1999	Scholastic
Robinson, Fay	Amazing Lizards	1999	Scholastic
Schwartz, David M.	If You Made a Million	1994	William Morrow
Sierra, Judy	Counting Crocodiles	1997	Singapore: Gulliver
Silverstein, Shel	The Giving Tree	1964	HarperCollins

Smith, Jodene Lynn	*Cut and Paste Science*	2003	Teacher Created
Stein, Sara	*The Evolution*	1986	Workman
Stenmark, Jean Kerr, Virginia Thompson, and Ruth Cossey	*Family Math*	1986	Regents, Univ. Calif.
Stickland, Paul	*Dinosaur Stomp*	1996	Dutton
Sweeney, Joan	*Me and My Place in Space*	1998	Crown
Tattersall, Clare	*Young Zillionaire's Guide to Money and Banking*	2000	Rosen
Thaler, Mike, and Jarad Lee	*The Math Teacher from the Black Lagoon*	1989	Scholastic
Viorst, Judith	*Alexander Who Used to Be Rich Last Sunday*	1980	Simon & Schuster
Vonderman, Carol	*How Math Works: 100 Ways Parents and Kids Can Share the Wonder of Mathematics*	1999	Putman
Wade, Lee	*The Cheerios Play Book*	1998	Simon and Schuster
Walsh, Ellen Stoll	*Mouse Count*	1991	Harcourt, Brace Jovanovich
Weidner-Zoehfeld, Kathleen	*Let's Read and Find Out Science Stage 2 Series*	1998	HarperCollins
Wiese, Jim	*Ancient Egypt*	2003	John Wiley & Sons
Wright, Alexandra	*Alice in Pastaland: A Math Adventure*	1997	Charlebridge
Wyatt, Valerie	*The Math Book for Girls and Other Beings Who Count*	2000	Kids Can Press

MIDDLE SCHOOL BOOKS

Author	Title	Copyright	Publisher
Accorsi, William	*Rachel Carson*	1993	Holiday House
Adams, Douglas	*Life, the Universe and Everything*	1986	Random House Value
Asimov, Isaac	*Extraterrestrial Civilizations*	1979	Crown
Asimov, Isaac	*Fantastic Voyage*	1966	Bantam
Asimov, Isaac	*I, Robot*	1983	Bantam

Asimov, Isaac	*Science Fiction, Science Fact*	1962	Mercury Press
Bauer, Joan	*Sticks*	1996	Bantam Doubleday
Bendick, Jeanne	*Along Came Galileo*	1999	Beautiful Feet
Berman, Bob	*Secrets of the Night Sky: Most Amazing Things in the Universe You Can See with the Naked Eye*	1996	Perennial: Harper
Bradbury, Ray	*The Martian Chronicles: The Grand Master Editions*	1979	Bantam Books
Brown, Jordan	*Elizabeth Blackwell*	1989	Chelsea House
Brunetto, Carolyn Ford	*Mathart*	1997	Scholastic
Bryce Walker	*Earthquake*	1982	Time-Life
Campbell, Robin	*Florence Sabin: Scientist*	1995	Chelsea House
Card, Orson Scott	*Ender's Game*	1994	Tor
Challoner, Jack	*Rocks and Minerals*	2002	Sagebrush Ed.
Cousins, Margaret	*Story of Thomas Alva Edison*	1965, 1981	Random House
Crichton, Michael	*Jurassic Park*	1990	Ballantine
Davies, Peter	*Inside the Hurricane*	2000	Henry Holt & Co.
Halam, Ann	*Dr. Franklin's Island*	2003	Laurel Leaf
Farmer, Nancy	*The House of the Scorpion*	2002	Scholastic
Glenn, William	*Earth, Wind, and Sky! Natural Science Lessons (Physics & Astronomy) for Gifted Students, Upper Elementary —Middle School*	1994	Gifted Education
Goodall, Jane	*In the Shadow of Man*	1988	Houghton Mifflin
Green, Jen	*Learn about Birds*	1997	National Book
Green, Jen	*Insects*	2000	Southwater
Green, Jen	*Rain Forests*	1999	Gareth Stevens
Greene, Thomas F.	*Marine Science*	1998	Amsco School
Grinstein, Louise S. and Paul Campbell	*Women of Mathematics: A Bibliographical Sourcebook*	1987	Greenwood
Haddix, Margaret Peterson	*Turnabout*	2000	Simmon
Herion, Claudia	*Women in Mathematics: The Addition of*	1997	Rutgers University

	Difference (Race, Gender and Science)		
Hickam, Homer	*October Sky*	1998	Random House
Holmes, Burnham	*George Eastman*	1992	Silver Burdett Printers
Isdell, Wendy, and Norton Juster	*The Dot and the Line: A Romance in Lower Mathematics*	2001	Chronicle Pub.
Kerrod, Robin	*Astronomy*	1998	Gareth Stevens Pub.
Kerrod, Robin	*Sea*	1997	Gareth Stevens Pub.
Kerrod, Robin	*Weather*	1998	Gareth Stevens Pub.
Klare, Roger	*Gregor Mendel*	1997	Enslow Publishing
Knutson, Roger	*Fearsome Fauna: A Field Guide to the Creatures That Live in You*	1999	W.H. Freeman
Krensky, Stephen	*Four against the Odds: The Struggle to Save Our Environment*	1992	Scholastic
Lasky, Kathryn	*Star Split*	2001	General
Lee, Martin, and Marcia Miller	*Mega-Fun Fractions*	2002	Scholastic
Markham, Lois	*Jacques-Yves Cousteau: Exploring the Wonders of the Sea*	1997	Stech Vaughn
Marsh, Carole	*Math for Girls: The Book with the Number on Getting Girls to Love and Excel in Math!*	1994	Gallopade Intl.
McGrayne, Sharon B.	*Novel Prize Women in Science: Their Lives, Struggles, and Momentous Discoveries*	2001	Joseph Henry
Mellett, Peter	*Pyramids*	1999	Gareth Stevens Pub.
Muschla, Judith A., and Gary Robert Muschla	*Math Smart*	2001	Wiley, John
Miller, Brendan, and Colleen Willard-Holt	*Dare to Differentiate: Content-Based Enrichment Strategies (Biology)*	2000	Gifted Education
Pappas, Theoni	*The Adventures of Penrose the Mathematical Cat*	1997	Wide World Pub.

Parker, Steve	The Human Body	1996	Franklin Watts
Parker, Steve	Guglielmo Marconi and Radio	1994	Chelsea House Pub.
Parker, Steve	Magnets	2002	Sagebrush Ed. Res.
Perl, Teri	Math Equals: Biographies of Women Mathematicians Plus Related Activities	1990	Addison-Wesley
Poynter, Margaret	Leakeys: Uncovering the Origins of Humankind	2001	Enslow
Sciezska, Jon, and Lane Smith	Math Curse	1995	Viking
Scieszka, Jon, and Lane Smith	Science Curse	2004	Viking
Singleton, Linda Joy	Regeneration	2001	Berkley Publishing
Sganga, Francis T.	Essentials for Mathematics for Gifted Students: Prep. for Algebra Grades 4–8.	2002	Gifted Education
Taiz, Lincoln	Libra: The Cat Who Saved Silicon Valley	2002	Amesa Group
Tobias, Sheila	Succeed with Math	1987	College Entrance
Vande, Velde	Heir Apparent	2002	Harcourt
Wade, Mary Dodson	Ada Byron Lovelace	1994	Silver Burdett
Walker, Bryce	Earthquake	1982	Time-Life
Werlin, Nancy	Double Helix	2004	Dial
Wheeler, Leslie	Rachel Carson	1991	Silver Burdett

HIGH SCHOOL BOOKS

Author	Title	Copyright	Publisher
Abbot, Edwin	Flat Land: A Romance of Dimensions	1991	Dover Publications
Adams, Douglas	The Hitchhiker's Guide to the Galaxy	1995	Ballantine
Aibek, Ken	Biohazard	1999	Dell
Anderson, Margaret	Carl Linneaus: Father of Classification	2001	Enslow
Anderson, Margaret	Charles Darwin	2001	Sagebrush Ed. Res.
Anderson, Margaret	Isaac Newton	1996	Enslow
Anderson, M.T.	Feed	2002	Candlewick

Armstong, Jennifer	*The Kiln*	2004	Eos
Avi	*The True Confessions of Charlotte Doyle*	1997	Harper Trophy
Bisson, Terry	*Miracle Man*	2001	Harper Entertainment
Bussing-Burks, Marie	*Young Zillionaire's Guide to Taxation and Government Spending*	2001	Rosen
Caes, Charles	*Young Zillionaire's Guide to the Stock Market*	2000	Rosen
Card, Orson Scott	*Masterpieces: The Best Science Fiction of the 20th Century*	2004	Ace
Cherryh, C. J.	*Voyager in Night*	1986	New American Lib.
Coville, Bruce	*I Lost My Grandfather's Brain*	1999	Aladdin
Cwiklik, Robert	*Albert Einstein and the Theory of Relativity*	1987	Barron's Publishing
Enzenberger, Hans	*The Number Devil: A Mathematical Adventure*	2000	Metropolitian
Flowers, Charles	*A Science Odyssey—100 Years of Discovery*	1998	William Morris & Co.
Freedman, Suzanne	*Dian Fossey: Befriending the Gorillas*	2000	Steck Vaugh Pub.
Gale, Christianson	*Isaac Newton*	1998	Sagebrush Ed. Res.
Gallo, Donald R.	*No Easy Answers*	1999	Laurel Leaf
Goldenstern, Joyce	*Albert Einstein Physicist & Genius*	1995	Enslow Publishers
Goodall, Jane	*My Life with Chimpanzees*	1996	Aladdin
Green, Meg	*Young Zillionaire's Guide to Investments and Savings*	2000	Rosen
Guillemin, Jeanne	*Anthrax: The Investigation of a Deadly Outbreak*	1999	Univ. of Calif. Press
Guthrie, William	*Socrates*	1972	Cambridge Univ. Press
Heinlein, Robert	*The Number of the Beast*	1989	Fawcett
Hightower, Paul	*Galileo: Astronomer and Physicist*	1997	Enslow
Isdell, Wendy	*A Zebra Named Al*	1993	Free Spirit Publishing

Loggia, Wendy	*Crushing on You*	1998	Bantam
Ma, Barbara R.	*The Only Math Book You'll Ever Need*	1986	Facts on File
Macaulay, David	*The New Way Things Work*	1998	Houghton Mifflin Co.
Martin, Ann M.	*Stacey the Math Whiz*	1997	Apple
Mellett, Peter	*Flight*	1998	Gareth Stevens
Miller, Judith, Engelberg, Stephen, and William Broad	*Germs—Biological Weapons and America's Secret War*	2001	Simon and Schuster
Montgomery, Sy	*The Tarantula Scientist*	2004	Houghton Mifflin
Moore, Emily	*Whose Side Are You On?*	1999	Sagebrush Education
Moriarty, Laura	*The Center of Everything*	2003	Hyperion
Namioka, Lensey	*Who's Hu?*	1981	Random House
Nielson, Jerry, and Maryanne Vollers	*Ice Bound*	2001	Hyperion
Owen, David	*Hidden Evidence*	2000	Quintet Publishing
Pasachoff, Naomi	*Marie Curie and the Science of Radioactivity*	1997	Sagebrush Ed. Res.
Patent, Dorothy Hinshaw	*Life in a Grassland*	2002	Lerner
Pevsner, Stella	*A Smart Kid Like You*	1983	Scholastic
Preston, Richard	*The Demon in the Freezer*	2002	Random House
Preston, Richard	*The Hot Zone*	1994	Anchor
Raymo, Chet	*365 Starry Nights: An Introduction to Astronomy for Every Night of the Year*	1982	Prentice Hall
Ridgway, Tom	*Young Zillionaire's Guide to Buying Goods And Services*	2000	Rosen
Ritchie, Alan	*Erin McEwan, Your Days Are Numbered*	1990	Random House
Robbins, Ken	*Autumn Leaves*	1998	Scholastic
Roberts, Jack	*The Importance of Dian Fossey*	1995	Lucent
Roberts, Royston	*Serendipity: Accidental Discoveries in Science*	1989	Wiley Science Ed.
Ruckman, Ivy	*Night of the Twisters*	1984	HarperCollins
Seidman, David	*Young Zillionaire's Guide to Supply and Demand*	2000	Rosen
Shull, Magan Elizabeth	*Yours Truly, Sky O'Shea*	2003	American Girl
Sobey, Ed	*Inventing Stuff*	1996	Dale Seymour Pub.

Stine, R. L.	*The Cheater*	1993	Simon Pulse
Stine, R. L.	*Night Games*	1996	Simon Pulse
Stefoff, Rebecca	*Charles Darwin*	1996	Oxford University
Taormino, Tristan	*A Girl's Guide to Taking Over the World*	1997	St. Martin's
Warriner, Holly	*Julian's Jinx*	1998	Aladdin
Wilson, Antoine	*Young Zillionaire's Guide to Distributing Goods and Services*	2001	Rosen

APPENDIX D: ORGANIZATIONS

American Association for the Advancement of Science (AAAS)
1200 New York Avenue, N.W.
Washington, DC 20005
(202) 326-6400
e-mail: webmaster@aaas.org
Website: www.aaas.org

Jets, Inc. (Junior Engineering Technical Society)
1420 King Street, Suite 405
Alexandria, VA 22314-2794
(703) 292-5111
e-mail: jets@nae.edu
Website: www.jets.org

National Science Foundation
4201 Wilson Blvd.
Arlington, VA 22230
(703) 292-5111
e-mail: infor@nsf.gov
Website: www.nsf.gov

American Association for Gifted Children
The AAGC is the nation's oldest advocacy organization for gifted
   children. It was established in the late 1940s.

American Association for Gifted Children at Duke University
Box 90270
Durham, NC 27708-0270
Website: www.aagc.org

The Association for the Gifted (TAG)
A special interest group of the Council for Exceptional Children (CEC)
1110 North Glebe Road
Suite 300
Arlington, VA 22201-5704
Website: www.cec.sped.org

The Connie Belin and Jacqueline N. Blank International Center for
    Gifted Education and Talent Development
The University of Iowa
210 Lindquist Center
Iowa City, IA 52242-1529
Website: http://uiowa.edu/~belinctr

The Halbert and Nancy Robinson Center for Young Scholars
University of Washington
Box 351630
Seattle, WA 98195-1630
Email: cscy@u.washington.edu
Website: http://depts.washington.edu/cscy

Hollingworth Center for Highly Gifted Children
827 Center Avenue #282
Dover, NH 03820-2506
Website: www.hollingworth.org

The National Foundation for Gifted and Creative Children
395 Diamond Hill Road
Warwick, RI 02886
Website: www.nfgcc.org

National Conference of Governor's Schools
c/o James Bray
Governor's School of West NC
2454 Lyndurst Avenue
Winston-Salem, NC 27103
Website: http://ncogs.org/

Teachers and Parents (TAP) for Bright Children
A division of Giftedness Quebec
McGill University
3700 McTavish Street
Montréal, Quebec H3A 1Y2
Canada
Tel: (514) 398-4252

APPENDIX E: MAGAZINES

Several magazines will publish the work of young authors. Although these are not specific to math and science, success often breeds success, and accomplishment in one academic arena will commonly elevate student achievement in general. In addition, integrating writing skills with math and science (e.g., science fiction writing) can open new perspectives for students.

Cricket Magazine Group: *Babybug* (ages 6 mos.–3 years), *Ladybug* (ages 3–6), *Spider* (ages 6–9), *Cricket* (ages 9–14), and *Cicada* (teens) (www.cricketmag.com/kids_home.asp)

Skipping Stones Magazine (international/multicultural) (www.skippingstones.org)

Young Writer Online (ages 5–18) (www.mystworld.com/youngwriter)

Potato Hill Poetry (grade K–12) (www.potatohill.com)

Stone Soup Magazine (up to age 13) (www.stonesoup.com)

Merlyn's Pen (grade 6–12) (www.merlynspen.org)

The Writer's Slate (grade K–12) (www.writingconference.com)

MidLink Magazine (ages 8–18) (www.ncsu.edu/midlink)

Potluck Children's Literary Magazine (ages 8–16) (http://hometown.aol.com/nappic)

APPENDIX F: SPECIAL PROGRAMS

Duke Action Science Camp for Young Women
Duke University
Durham, North Carolina
A unique and exciting summer program for young women in middle school who are interested in science and would enjoy an intensive learning experience filled with discovery. The camp is designed to build upon campers' existing science skills, promote an understanding and appreciation of environmental issues, and develop confidence through activity-centered learning.
203 Bishop's House
Box 90702
Durham, NC 27708
(919) 684-2827
Fax: (919) 681-8235
e-mail: dukeyouth@duke.edu
Website: www.learnmore.duke.edu/Youth/act/index.htm

Nurturing Nature and Numbers
Maine School of Science and Mathematics
Limestone, Maine
This camp is focused on science, math, and computers for middle-school girls, grades 5–8
Camp Co-Director
Maine School of Science and Mathematics

95 High Street
Limestone, ME 04750
(800) 325-4484
Fax: (207) 325-3340
e-mail: nnn@mssm.org
Website: www.mssm.org/nnn

Science Quest
Seton Hill College
Greensburg, Pennsylvania
A residential summer camp for girls in grades 7–12 interested in
math, science, and computers.
Science Quest Director
Seton Hill College
Greensburg, PA 15601
(724) 834-2200
Fax: (724) 830-1294
e-mail: vochum@setonhill.edu
Website: www.maura.setonhill.edu/~msct/camp/index.htm

APPENDIX G: STATE ORGANIZATIONS FOR THE GIFTED

- Alabama
  - Alabama Association for Gifted Children
    http://http://www.aagc.freeservers.com/aagc.html
- Arizona
  - Arizona Association for Gifted and Talented
    http://www.azagt.org
- Arkansas
  - Arkansans for Gifted and Talented Education
    http://agate.k12.ar.us/
- California
  - California Association for the Gifted (CAG)
    http://www.CAGifted.org
- Colorado
  - Colorado Association for the Gifted
    http://www.cde.state.co.us/cdeedserv/gtactsh.htm
    email: CAGT@aol.com
- Connecticut
  - Connecticut Association for the Gifted and Talented
    http://www.ctgifted.org
- Florida
  - Florida Association for the Gifted (FLAG) and
    Parents for Able Learner Students
    http://www.flagifted.org

- Georgia
  - Georgia Association for Gifted Children
    http://www.gagc.org
- Hawaii
  - Hawaii Gifted Association
    http://www.k12.hi.us/~gtstate/Index.htm
- Idaho
  - Idaho—The Association for the Gifted (ITAG)
    www.itag-sage.org
- Illinois
  - Illinois Association for Gifted Children (IAGC)
    http://IAGCGifted.org
- Indiana
  - Indiana Association for the Gifted
    http://www.iag-online.org
- Iowa
  - Iowa Talented and Gifted Association
    http://www.uiowa.edu/~itag
- Kansas
  - Kansas Association for the Gifted, Talented and Creative
    http://www.KGTC.org
- Kentucky
  - Kentucky Association for Gifted Education (KAGE)
    http://www.wku.edu/KAGE
- Louisiana
  - Association for Gifted and Talented Students (AGTS)
    http://hal.calc.k12.la.us/~gifted/gifted.html
- Maine
  - Maine Educators Gifted and Talented (MEGAT)
    http://www.sad28.k12.me.us
- Maryland
  - Maryland Coalition for Gifted & Talented Education (MC-GATE)
    http://www.howardK12.md.us/gtp/statcnf1.html
- Massachusetts
  - Massachusetts Association for Gifted Education (MAGE)
    http://www.MASSGifted.org

- Michigan
    - Michigan Alliance for Gifted Education (MAGE)
      http://www.migiftedchild.org
- Minnesota
    - Minnesota Council for the Gifted and Talented
      http://www.MCGT.net
      Minnesota Educators of the Gifted and Talented
      http://www.informns.k12.us/~megt
- Mississippi
    - Mississippi Association for Gifted Children (MAGC)
      http://www.magc.org
- Missouri
    - Gifted Association of Missouri (GAM)
      http://www.mogam.org
- Montana
    - Montana Association of Gifted and Talented Education
      http://www.members.home.net/cabreras/agate.htm
- Nebraska
    - Nebraska Association for the Gifted
      http://www.NebraskaGifted.org
- New Hampshire
    - New Hampshire Association for Gifted Children
      http://www.nhage.org
- New Jersey
    - New Jersey Association for Gifted Children
      http://www.NJAGC.org
- New York
    - Advocacy for Gifted and Talented Education in New York, USA
      (AGATE)
      http://www.agateny.org
- North Carolina
    - North Carolina Association for the Gifted and Talented
      (NCAGT)
      http://www.ncagt.org
- Ohio
    - Ohio Association for Gifted Children (OAGC)
      http://www.oagc.com

- Oklahoma
    - Oklahoma Association for Gifted, Creative and Talented
      http://www.title3.sde.state/ok.us/gifted
- Oregon
    - Oregon Association for Talented & Gifted (OATAG)
      http://www.oatag.org
- Pennsylvania
    - Pennsylvania Association for Gifted Education (PAGE)
      http://www.penngifted.org
- Rhode Island
    - Rhode Island-Gifted and Talented
      http://www.ri.net/gifted_talented/rhode.html
- South Carolina
    - South Carolina Consortium Gifted Education
      http://www.SCCGE.org
- South Dakota
    - South Dakota Association for Gifted Education
      http://www.sd-age.org
- Tennessee
    - Tennessee Association for the Gifted (TAG)
      http://www.tag-tenn.org
- Texas
    - Texas Association for the Gifted and Talented (TAGT)
      http://www.txgifted.org
- Utah
    - Utah Association for Gifted Children (UAGC)
      http://www.uagc.org
- Vermont
    - Vermont Council for Gifted
      http://www.vcge.org
- Virginia
    - Virginia Association of the Gifted (VAG)
      http://www.vagifted.org
- Washington
    - Washington Association of Educators of the Talented and Gifted
      (WAETG)
      http://www.waetag.org

- West Virginia
  - West Virginia Association for Gifted and Talented
    http://www.wvgifted.org
- Wisconsin
  - Wisconsin Association for Gifted and Talented (WATG)
    http://www.focol.org/~watg

APPENDIX H: STATE DEPARTMENT OF EDUCATION GIFTED EDUCATION CONTACTS

Alabama Department of Education
P. O. Box 302101
Montgomery, AL 36130-2101
(334) 242-8114
(334) 242-9192 (fax)

Alaska Department of Education & Early Development
801 West 10th St., Suite 200
Juneau, AK 99801
(907) 465-8727
(907) 465-6760 (fax)

Arizona Department of Education
1535 West Jefferson
Phoenix, AZ 85007
(602) 364-4017
(602) 542-3100 (fax)

Arkansas Department of Education
Education Bldg., Room 203-B
4 State Capitol Mall
Little Rock, AR 72201

(501) 682-4224
(501) 682-4220 (fax)

California Department of Education
1430 N Street, Suite 2401
Sacramento, CA 95814
(916) 323-5505

Colorado Department of Education
201 East Colfax Avenue
Denver, CO 80203-1799
(303) 866-6652
(303) 866-6811 (fax)

Connecticut Department of Education
165 Capitol Avenue, Rm. 205
Hartford, CT 06106
(860) 713-6745
(860) 713-7018 (fax)

Delaware Department of Public Instruction
P. O. Box 1402
Townsend Building
Dover, DE 19903
(302) 739-4885, ext. 3145
(302) 739-4675 (fax)

Florida Department of Education
614 Turlington Building
325 W. Gaines Street
Tallahassee, FL 32399-0400
(850) 245-0478
(850) 922-7088 (fax)

Georgia Department of Education
1770 Twin Towers East
Atlanta, GA 30334-5040

(404) 657-0182
(404) 657-7096 (fax)

Guam Department of Education
P. O. Box DL
Hagatna, Guam 96932
(671) 475-0598

Hawaii Department of Education
637 18th Avenue, Bldg. C, #204
Honolulu, HI 96816
(808) 733-4476
(808) 733-4475 (fax)

Iowa Department of Education
Grimes State Office Building
East 14th & Grand
Des Moines, IA 50319-0146
(515) 281-3199
(515) 242-6025 (fax)

Idaho Department of Education
P. O. Box 83720
Boise, ID 83720-0027
(208) 332-6800

Illinois Board of Education
100 North First Street #205
Springfield, IL 62777
(866) 262-6663

Indiana Department of Education
Room 229, State House
Indianapolis, IN 46204
(317) 233-5191
(317) 232-9121 (fax)

Kansas Department of Education
120 SE 10th Street
Topeka, KS 66612
(785) 291-3097
(785) 296-1413 (fax)

Kentucky Department of Education
Division of Professional Development
500 Mero St., Rm. 1835
Frankfort, KY 40601
(502) 564-4770

Louisiana Department of Education
1453 Patrick Drive
Baton Rouge, LA 70810
(225) 342-5295
(225) 342-3281 (fax)

Massachusetts Department of Education
350 Main Street
Malden, MA 02148
(781) 338-6239

Maryland Department of Education
200 West Baltimore Street
Baltimore, MD 21201-2595
(410) 767-0363
(410) 333-2050 (fax)

Maine Department of Education
23 State House Station
Augusta, ME 04333
(207) 624-6831
(207) 624-6821 (fax)

Michigan Department of Education
P. O. Box 30008

Lansing, MI 48909
(517) 373-4213
(517) 241-0197 (fax)

Minnesota Department of Education
1500 Hwy 36 West
Roseville, MN 55113-4266
(651) 582-8200

Missouri Dept. of Elementary & Secondary Education
P. O. Box 480
Jefferson City, MO 65102
(573) 751-2453
(573) 751-9434 (fax)

Mississippi Department of Education
Office of Deputy Superintendent
P. O. Box 771
Jackson, MS 39205-0771
(601) 359-2588
(601) 359-2326 (fax)

Montana Office of Public Instruction
P. O. Box 202501
Helena, MT 59620-2501
(406) 444-4317
(406) 444-1373 (fax)

Nebraska Department of Education
301 Centennial Mall South, Box 94987
Lincoln, NE 68509-4987
(402) 471-0737
(402) 471-8850 (fax)

New Hampshire Department of Education
101 Pleasant Street
Concord, NH 03301

(603) 271-1536
(603) 271-1953 (fax)

New Jersey Department of Education
Legge House, Normal Avenue
Montclair State University
Upper Montclair, NJ 07043
(973) 569-2113

New Mexico Department of Education
300 Don Gaspar
Santa Fe, NM 87501
(505) 827-6653
(505) 827-6791(fax)

Nevada Department of Education
700 E. Fifth St.
Carson City, NV 89701
(775) 687-9142
(775) 775-9101

New York State Summer Institutes
N.Y. State Education Department
Room 981 EBA
Washington Avenue
Albany, NY 12234
(518) 474-8773

North Carolina Department of Public Instruction
6356 Mail Service Center
Raleigh, NC 27699-6356
(919) 807-3987
(919) 807-3243 (fax)

North Dakota Department of Public Instruction
State Univ. Station Box 5036
Fargo, ND 58105-5036
(701) 231-6030

Ohio Department of Education
25 S. Front Street
Mailstop 205
Columbus, OH 43215
(614) 752-1221
(614) 752-1429 (fax)

Oklahoma Department of Education
2500 N. Lincoln Blvd.
Suite 316
Oklahoma City, OK 73105-4599
(405) 521-4287
(405) 521-2971 (fax)

Oregon Department of Education
255 Capitol St., N.E.
Salem, OR 97310-0290
(503) 378-3569
(503) 378-5156 (fax)

Pennsylvania Department of Education
Bureau of Special Education, 7th Floor
333 Market Street
Harrisburg, PA 17126-0333
(717) 783-6881

Rhode Island Dept. of Elementary & Secondary Education
255 Westminister St., Room 400
Providence, RI 02903-3400
(401) 222-4600, ext. 2318
(401) 222-6030 (fax)

South Carolina Department of Education
1429 Senate Street, Rm. 801
Columbia, SC 29201
(803) 734-8335
(803) 734-6142 (fax)

South Dakota Department of Education
700 Governors Drive
Pierre, SD 57501-2291
(605) 773-4662
(605) 773-3782 (fax)

Tennessee Department of Education
Division of Special Education
710 James Robertson Pkwy, 8th Floor
Nashville, TN 37243-0380
(615) 741-7811
(615) 532-9412 (fax)

Texas Education Agency
1701 N. Congress Avenue
Austin, TX 78701-1494
(512) 463-9455

Utah Office of Education
P.O. Box 144200
Salt Lake City, UT 84114-4200
(801) 538-7884
(801) 538-7769 (fax)

Vermont Department of Education
120 State Street
Montpelier, VT 05620-2501
(802) 828-5411

Virginia Department of Education
Office of Elementary & Middle School
P. O. Box 2120
Richmond, VA 23218-2120
(804) 225-2884
(804) 786-1703 (fax)

Washington Office of Public Instruction
P. O. Box 47200

600 South Washington
Olympia, WA 98504-7200
(360) 725-6100
(360) 586-3305 (fax)

Washington D.C. Public Schools
825 N Capitol St., N.E., Rm 8084
Washington, DC 20002
(202) 442-5650

Wisconsin Department of Public Instruction
P.O. Box 7841
Madison, WI 53707
(615) 266-2364

West Virginia Department of Education
Capitol Complex
Building 6, Room 304
Charleston, WV 25305
(304) 558-2696
(304) 558-3741 (fax)

Wyoming Department of Education
Hathaway Building, 2nd Floor
2300 Capitol Avenue
Cheyenne, WY 82002
(307) 777-5217

APPENDIX I: WEBSITES FOR PARENTS, TEACHERS, AND STUDENTS

We suggest the following websites as good starting points for parents, teachers, and students. Many of them provide opportunities for community involvement, and several are particularly useful toward the design of classroom projects.

The Council for Exceptional Children (CEC) is the largest international professional organization dedicated to improving educational outcomes for individuals with exceptionalities, students with disabilities, and/or the gifted.
Website: www.cec.sped.org/index.html

American Regions Mathematics League (ARML)
Website: www.arml.com

The Association for the Gifted (TAG) was organized as a division of the Council for Exceptional Children in 1958 to help both professionals and parents deal more effectively with the gifted child.
Website: www.cectag.org

Ecokids Online
This education website provides information and interesting facts about the environment via games and activities. Geared for children, the site encourages children to think for themselves, formulate opinions, make

decisions, and understand the impact their own actions have on the environment. There is plenty of information for parents and teachers as well on this site.
Website: http://ecokids.earthday.ca/pub/index.cfm

The ERIC Clearinghouse on Disabilities and Gifted Education is part of the National Library of Education (NLE), Office of Educational Research and Improvement (OERI), and the U.S. Department of Education. ERIC is operated by the Council for Exceptional Children (CEC) and provides information on a wide variety of education topics such as ADD, gifted, behavior disorders, early childhood, inclusion, and learning disabilities.
Website: http://ericec.org/gifted/gt-menu.html

The National Association for Gifted Children (NAGC) is an organization of parents, educators, other professionals, and community leaders to address the unique needs of children and youth with demonstrated gifts and talents as well as those children who may be able to develop their talent potential with appropriate educational experiences.
Website: www.nagc.org

Supporting Emotional Needs of the Gifted (SENG) focuses primarily on the adults in the lives of gifted children. SENG provides information on identification, guidance, and effective ways to live and work with gifted individuals.
Website: www.SENGifted.org

The National Parent Information Network (NPIN) is a project of the ERIC system and is administered by the National Library of Education and the U.S. Department of Education. The mission of NPIN is to provide access to research-based information about the process of parenting and about family involvement in education.
Website: http://npin.org

Hoagies' Gifted Education Page is a resource guide for the education of gifted children with links to resources on nearly every aspect of gifted education available on the Internet, plus annotations and firsthand information provided by parents.
Website: www.hoagiesgifted.org

Gifted-Children.com: Identification, Encouragement, and Development (GCC) is an online parents' newsletter with networking and information dedicated to making a difference in the education of children with special talents and abilities.
Website: www.gifted-children.com

GT World is an online support community for parents of gifted and talented children.
Website: www.gtworld.org/index.html

The Gifted Development Center provides parents, schools, and advocacy groups with information about identification, assessment, counseling, learning styles, programs, presentations, and resources for gifted children and adults.
Website: www.gifteddevelopment.com

Davidson Institute for Talent Development is currently one of only two national foundations supporting the profoundly gifted population. The Davidson Institute's mission is to recognize, nurture, and support profoundly gifted young people and to provide opportunities for them to develop their talents in positive ways to create value for themselves and others.
Website: www.davidsoninstitute.org

Education Program for Gifted Youth at Stanford University is a continuing project dedicated to developing and offering multimedia computerized distance-learning courses. Through EPGY, students have access to courses in a variety of subjects at levels ranging from kindergarten through advanced undergraduate. Currently over 3,000 students from twenty-eight countries are enrolled in EPGY.
Website: www-epgy.stanford.edu/:EPGY

Hurricane Hunters has photos and information from the Hurricane Hunters of the Air Force Reserve. Take a "cyberflight" and follow them on a trip.
Website: www.hurricanehunters.com

Adopt-a-Pilot Program. What: Southwest Airlines' mentoring program that pairs pilots with fifth-grade pupils around the country, many in cities the airline doesn't serve. How: Pilots meet with pupils in the classroom and stay in touch during their travels. Who's eligible: The program is free.
Website: www.southwest.com/adoptapilot

Weather Wiz Kids is designed to give kids a look into the fascinating world of weather. Includes games, quizzes, and experiments you can do at home.
Website: www.weatherwizkids.com

GirlStart Organization encourages girls in math, science, and technology and offers games, postcards, career info, and advice.
Website: www.girlstart.org

Tomorrow's Girl Publisher is dedicated to fostering an interest science in girls, and features educational books for girls, news, and extensive links.
Website: www.tomorrows-girls.com

EGEMS—Electronic Games for Education in Math and Science—is a great site with examples of creative games for girls involving discrete math and computer science concepts.
Website: http://taz.cs.ubc.ca/egems/home.html

The Girl Scientist is a virtual community of girls who are into science, technology, and math and want to share what they are doing with fellow girls and female scientists around the world.
Website: www.girlscientist.org

Hypatia Institute is a website for gender equity in physics, astronomy, and science education.
Website: www.hypatiamaze.org

Discovery Channel School
Website: www.school.discovery.com

Eisenhower National Commission
Curriculum resources and useful information for math and science
teaching.
Website: www.enc.org

Exploring the Solar System
Website: www.nytimes.com/library/national science/solar-index.html

Junior Engineering Technical Society (JETS)
Website: www.jets.org

Mathematics Education at Northern Kentucky University
Website: www.nku.edu/~mathed/gifted.html

National Science Bowl
Website: www.scied.science.doe.gov/nsb

Science Olympiad
Website: www.soinc.org

USA Mathematical Talent Search (USAMTS)
Website: www.nas.gov/usamts

U.S. Physics Team
Website: www.aapt.org/contests/olympiad.cfm

Northwestern University Center for Talent Development Resources
Programs for middle and high school students. This informative website
includes a definition of distance learning, a list of special characteristics
required of the students, and recommendations for parents.
Website: www.ctd.northwestern.edu:16080/resources

Yahoo! Directory
Courses listed are for all age ranges, but are not specifically for gifted
students.
Website: http://dir.yahoo.com/Education/Distance_Learning/K_12

Virtual Schools: Trends and Issues: A Study of Virtual Schools in the United States—This study lists the trends for virtual schools and includes three pages of links to schools offering at least a partial K–12 curricula through web-based courses. This site should be a starting point for educators and administrators considering web-based instruction for their students. Included is an extensive list of recommendations, as well as survey of results from participating virtual schools.
Website: www.dlrn.org/virtualstudy.pdf

Windows to the Universe
This is a great site with plenty of interesting activities to choose from in the "Stuff to Do" menu, including guided tours, information on volcanoes, the solar system, earth, the physics of space, sun, space missions, just tons of information. Educators can also access various classroom activities in the teacher workbook. Educational games and guided tours make this site well worth looking at.
Website: www.windows.ucar.edu

Science Service
http://www.sciserv.org/
A time-tested, nonprofit organization based in Washington, DC, whose mission is to advance the understanding and appreciation of science. Their website provides several excellent links, including several to science competitions. The site also includes:

Science Training Programs
Website: www.sciserv.org/stp/
According to Science Service, this is "the only comprehensive catalog of science, mathematics and engineering enrichment programs for pre-college students and teachers."
NEC Extreme Science
Website: www.sciserv.org/necfoundation.asp
NEC Give a Day, Make a Difference, brings together middle-school students and teachers with some of America's most accomplished scientists and engineers.
NEC Perfect Classroom Competition is a national competition that will award three middle-school science teachers a total of $9,000 for

classroom improvements. Teachers are encouraged to submit video essays describing a vision for the perfect classroom.

Society for Amateur Scientists
A group that brings science and scientists in closer contact with the rest of society. There are plenty of opportunities here for involvement at all ages.
Website: www.sas.org/

Figure This
Endorsed by the National Council of Teachers of Mathematics, this website provides oodles of math challenges. There are also teacher and family "corners" that include homework tips.
Website: http://www.figurethis.org

Mu Alpha Theta
A nonprofit National Mathematics Honor Society dedicated to math and math education.
Website: www.mualphatheta.org

The Junior Engineering Technological Society
This is a great site for junior and senior high school students. In addition to other information that they might find useful, there is a section that invites students to take the "JETS challenge." A difficult math/engineering problem is presented and students have one week to come up with the right answer.
Website: www.jets.org

Classroom Earth
A collection of top-notch environmental education programs, and information on how to obtain materials and training related to environmental education. This site would be especially valuable in April, when classrooms throughout the country celebrate and actively support Earth Day!
Website: http://www.classroomearth.org/

Space Day, 101 Ways to Celebrate!
Teachers and students will find this site very helpful; each year focuses on a different interactive space theme.
Website: http://www.spaceday.org

Howard Hughes Medical Institute (HHMI)
HHMI provides a service in which it lists opportunities for elementary and secondary level students. Just scroll down the page and select that group under "opportunities for." Note that there is also a category for teachers that provides plenty of interesting opportunities for funding and ongoing education.
Website: www.hhmi.org/grants/reports/scienceopp/main

APPENDIX J: SCIENCE AND MATH COMPETITIONS

SCIENCE AND MATH COMPETITIONS THROUGHOUT THE UNITED STATES

Engaging in academic competitions can be a great experience for students, provided they keep healthy perspectives on the implications of "winning" and "losing." The process should serve to challenge them, boost their confidence, and provide them with opportunities to meet other students like themselves, in an atmosphere where academic achievement is respected and lauded. Of course, students tend to be more highly motivated if their participation is self-conceived, and is not seen as "homework." We urge you to offer these competitions as optional, free-time pursuits that are approached in a spirit of fun and adventure.

Most of these competitions combine accomplishment with the excitement of travel, as highly ranked students are usually asked to proceed to state and national levels. Several competitions also have international counterparts, which can be accessed through the national websites. Students who are ready for a greater challenge should consider applying for the national team in their discipline of choice (specifically, math, chemistry, physics, and computing).

Need help mentoring a science fair contestant? The Intel science fair site (www.sciserv.org/isef/primer) has useful tips for all science fairs. Just hunt around a bit. Also, the Society for Amateur Scientists gives advice at www.scifair.org/.

A very important idea to keep in mind: check with local or state teaching associations to find regional competitions and activities. You might be surprised by the opportunities that are in your own backyard! It is often as simple as typing the keywords "science," "competition," and the name of the nearest city into your favorite Internet search engine. Furthermore, remember to check other keywords that might lead you to more technically based competitions. There are some good ones for various types of engineering, automotive repair, technical design, drawing, writing, etc. Happy hunting!

Academic Decathlon
While this competition is not specific to science and math, we have included it on our list because it supports high standards for academic achievement, and exposes students to a diverse array of bright colleagues.
Website: www.usad.org/

American Computer Science League (ACSL)
Box 40118
Providence, RI 02940
(401) 822-4312
Website: www.acsl.org/acsl

The American Mathematics Competitions
A truly stellar site describing competitions for junior and senior high students! The Mathematical Association of America has been holding these competitions for more than fifty years, and is still going strong. The site also provides information on the Mathematical Olympiad Summer Program and much more.
University of Nebraska-Lincoln
Lincoln, NE 68588-0658
(402) 472-6566
Fax: (402) 472-6087
e-mail: titu@amc.unl.edu
Website: www.unl.edu/amc

Chemistry Olympiad
(The web address is rather long, you might just want to search the Internet for the term "Chemistry Olympiad" and click on the link provided). A high school, test-based competition for the serious chemistry student. This site also has links to study camps, mentors, and more.
Website:
www.chemistry.org/portal/a/c/s/1/acsdisplay.html?DOC = education%5Cstudent%5Colympiad.html

Computing Olympiad (USACO)
This site is sparser and a bit harder to navigate than the other Olympiad sites, but a few clicks will tell you what you need to know. There are several (four or five) competitions each year, and you only need Internet access to participate.
Website:
http://oldweb.uwp.edu/academic/mathematics/usaco/index.htm

The Craftsman/NSTA Young Inventors Awards Program
National Science Teachers Association
1840 Wilson Boulevard
Arlington, VA 22201-3000
(888) 494-4994
e-mail: youninventors@nsta.org
Website: www.nsta.org/programs/craftsman.htm

The Discovery Channel Young Scientist Challenge
A fantastic science contest for grades 5–8. Interestingly, students are judged not only on their scientific knowledge but also on their ability to effectively communicate scientific ideas.
Website: www.sciserv.org/dysc/

First Robotics Competition
FIRST
200 Bedford Street
Manchester, NH 03101
(800) 871-8326
Fax: (603) 666-3907
Website: www.usfirst.org

Intel International Science and Engineering Fair
Science Service
1719 N Street, NW
Washington, DC 20036
(202) 785-2255
Fax: (202) 785-1243
e-mail: sciedu@sciserv.org
Website: www.sciserv.org/itsef

International Mathematical Olympiad (IMO)
University of Nebraska
1740 Vine Street
Lincoln, NE 68588-0681
(888) 449-2001
e-mail: imo2001@amc.unl.edu
Website: http://imo2001.usa.unl.edu

International Physics Olympiad
Website: www.jyu.fi/tdk/kasdk/olympiads

Lemelson-MIT Inventeams
Fifteen high schools are awarded grants up to $10,000 every year so that
they may create a prototype of an invention that will solve a specific
problem.
Website: www.inventeams.org

Lucent's Technology Challenge
National Science Teachers Association
1840 Wilson Boulevard
Arlington, VA 22201-3000
(888) 255-4242
e-mail: lucent@nsta.org
Website: www.nsta.org/programs/lucent

Mathcounts
A series of competitions designed for grades 7–8. It is a four-stage, year-
long program run jointly by the National Society of Professional Engi-

neers, the National Council of Teachers of Mathematics, NASA, and the CAN Foundation.

Mathcounts Foundation
1420 King Street
Alexandria, VA 22314
(703) 684-2828
Fax: (703) 836-4875
e-mail: mathcounts@nspe.org
Website: www.mathcounts.org

Math League Contests
Math League Press
P. O. Box 17
Tenafly, NJ 07670-0017
(201) 568-6328
Fax: (201) 816-0125
Website: www.mathleague.com

National Science Olympiad
5955 Little Pine Lane
Rochester, MI 48306
(248) 651-4013
Fax: (248) 651-7835
e-mail: Sonic@sonic.org
Website: www.macomb.k12.mi.us/ims/cr/science/so/nsoly/index.htm

ROBOlinks
Maintained by Robotbooks.com, this site provides links to more than 50 competitions that take place around the globe!
Website: www.robotbooks.com/robot-competition-links.htm

Siemens Foundation (The Westinghouse Competition)
A classic and prestigious competition for original research projects in math, science, and technology at the high-school level.
Website: www.siemens-foundation.org/

The Junior Sciences and Humanities Symposium
Sponsored by the armed services, this competition strives to promote
research and experimentation in the sciences, engineering, and mathematics at the high school level, while emphasizing "humane and ethical
principles in the application of research results."
Website: www.jshs.org

USA Computing Olympiad
USACO
University of Wisconsin-Parkside
900 Wood Road
P. O. Box 2000
Kenosha, WI 53141-2000
(414) 595-2231
Fax: (414) 595-2056
e-mail: piele@cs.uwp.edu
Website: www.uwp.edu/academic/mathematics/usaco

American Regions Mathematics League (ARML)
An annual national mathematics competition for high school students.
ARML is held simultaneously at three sites: Penn State, the University
of Iowa, and San Jose State University.
Website: www.arml.com

Annual Math League Contests
Math League Press, Tenafly, NJ
Website: www.mathleague.com

MOEMS
Mathematical Olympiads for Elementary and Middle Schools, an in-
school academic year competition for students in 8th grade and
younger. There are two divisions: "E" for grades 4–6 and "M" for
grades 6–8.
Website: www.moems.org

National Ocean Science Bowl
High school teams compete in a knowledge-based, game-show–like format that focuses on ocean sciences. Because the questions cover biol-

ogy, physics, chemistry, geology, and other topics as well, teams are encouraged to include students from a diversity of scientific backgrounds.
Website: www.nosb.org/

National Science Bowl
Run by the Department of Energy, this quiz bowl competition also incorporates an engineering project if students reach the national level. It covers all scientific fields, so teams should be diverse in their knowledge!
Website: www.scied.science.doe.gov/nbs

Physics Bowl
A test-based competition for high school students, sponsored by the American Association of Physics Teachers. Participation takes very little effort.
Website: www.aapt.org/Contests/physicsbowl.cfm

U.S. Chemistry Team (High School)
American Chemical Society, Washington, DC
Website: www.acs.org/education/student/olympiad.html

U.S. Physics Team (High School)
American Association of Physics Teachers, American Center for Physics College Park, MD
Website: www.aapt.org/Contests/olympiad.cfm

CANADIAN COMPETITIONS

Various Canadian Competitions
This site, published by the University of Toronto, provides excellent "one-stop shopping" for several high-school competitions.
Website: www.biocomp.utoronto.ca/otherexams/

Canadian Mathematical Society
A comprehensive site for mathematics throughout Canada.
Website: www.cms.math.ca/

Need help mentoring a science fair contestant? There's plenty of helpful information for regional and national Canadian science fairs at this site.
Website: www.cdli.ca/sciencefairs/

BIBLIOGRAPHY

Allen, R., H. Gale, and C. Skitl. 1994. *Mighty mindbenders*. Austin, Tex.: Barnes and Noble.

Assouline, S., and A. Lupkowski-Schoplick. 2003. *Developing mathematical talent: A guide for challenging and educating gifted students*. Waco, Tex.: Prufrock Press.

Benbow, C., and L. Minor. Cognitive profiles of verbally and mathematically precocious students. *Gifted Child Quarterly* 34, no. 1 (1990): 21–26.

Betts, G. T., and J. K. Kercher. 1999. *The autonomous learner model: Optimizing ability*. Greeley, Colo.: ALPS

Bloom, B. S., ed. 1956. *Taxonomy of educational objectives: The classification of educational goals. Handbook I: The cognitive domain*. New York: David McKay.

Burns, L. M. 1993. *Meadow: An integrated system for intelligent tutoring of subtraction concepts and procedure*. New York: Columbia University.

Callard-Szulgit, R. 2003 *Perfectionism and gifted children*. Lanham, Md: Scarecrow Press.

Campbell, J. R. Secrets of award-winning programs for gifted in mathematics. *Gifted Child Quarterly* 32, no. 4 (1988): 326–65.

Carson, R. 1961. *The Sea around us*. New York: Oxford University Press.

Colangelo, N., S. Assouline, and M. Gross. 2004. *A nation deceived: How schools hold back America's brightest students*. Vol. 1. Iowa City: University of Iowa.

Conrad, S. and D. Flegler. 1993. *Math contest: Grade 7 and 8 and algebra course 1*. Tenafly, N.J.: Math League Press.

Csikszentmihalyi, M. 1990. *FLOW: The psychology of optimal experience*. New York: Harper and Row.

Davidson, J., and B. Davidson. 2004. *Genius denied*. New York: Simon and Schuster.

Davis, R. B. 1964. *Discovery in mathematics*. Palo Alto, Calif.: Addison-Wesley.

Eiber, C. R. 1987. The North Carolina School of Science and Mathematics. *Phi Delta Kappan* 68 (June): 773–77.

Flanders, J. R. 1987. How much of the content in mathematics textbooks is new? *Arithmetic Teacher* 35 no. 1:18–23.

Ginsburg, H. P. 1987. *Assessing the arithmetic abilities and instructional needs of students*. Austin, Tex.: Pro-Ed.

Goldenberg, L., H. Ba, J. Heinze, and A. Hess. (2003). "JASON multimedia science curriculum impact on student learning: Final evaluation report." New York: Center of Children and Technology, Education Development Center.

Goleman, D. 1995. *Emotional intelligence*. New York: Bantam.

Howe, J. M A. 1999. *Genius explained*. Cambridge, Mass.: Cambridge University Press.

Karnes, F., and K. Stephens. 2002. *Young women of achievement*. Amherst, N.Y.: Prometheus Books.

Kirby, B. 2005. What is Asperger's? http://www.udel.edu/bkirby/asperger/aswhatisit.html

Little, C. 2002. Which is it? Asperger's syndrome or giftedness: Defining the differences. *Gifted Child Today* (winter): 58–63.

Odyssey of the Mind. 2003–2004. *Odyssey of the Mind: a long-term problem synopsis* at www.odysseyofthemind.com/materials/2004synopsis1.php (accessed March 7, 2004).

Ross, P., ed. 1993. *National excellence: A case for developing America's talent*. Washington, D.C.: U.S. Department of Education.

Schooler, L. J., and J. R. Anderson. 1990. *The disruptive potential of immediate feedback*. Proceedings of twelfth Cognitive Science Conference, Cambridge, Mass., 702–8.

Silverman, L. K. 1998. Personality and learning styles of gifted children. In *Excellence in educating gifted and talented learners*, 3rd ed, edited by J. Van-Tassel-Baska, 29–65. Denver: Love.

Stanley, J. C., and C. D. Benbow. 1983. Educating mathematically precocious youths: Twelve policy recommendations. *Educational Researcher* 11, no. 5: 4–9.

Subotnik, R. F. 1988. Factors from the structure of intellect model associated with gifted adolescents' problem finding in science: research with Westinghouse Science Talent Search winners. *Journal of Creative Behaviors* 22, no. 1: 42–54.

Treffinger, D., K. Dorval, and S. Isaksen. 2000. *Creative problem solving*, 3rd ed. Waco, Tex.: Prufrock Press.

Treffinger, D. 2003. *Independent, self-directed learning: 2003 update*. Sarasota, Fla.: Center for Creative Learning.

Torrance, E. P. and H. T. Safter 1990. *The incubation model of teaching: Getting beyond the aha!* Buffalo, N.Y.: Creative Education Foundation Press.

Wickelgren, W. A., and I. Wickelgren. 2001. *Math coach: A parent's guide to helping children succeed in math*. New York: Berkley Books.

ABOUT THE AUTHORS

Dr. Rosemary Callard-Szulgit has 37 years of teaching experience and counseling working with gifted children, their parents and other educators, devoting her entire career to the fair and equitable education of all children.

As an associate faculty at the State University of New York College at Brockport, Rosemary continues with her very popular and well-respected courses in Gifted Studies. She was also the former Coordinator for Gifted Studies in a large suburban school district in Rochester, New York. Rosemary has spoken extensively both nationally and internationally and continues her staff development trainings with school districts throughout the United States. She is listed in *Who's Who Among American Educators*.

Dr. Callard-Szulgit has written three other books, *Parenting and Teaching the Gifted*, *Perfectionism and Gifted Children*, and *Teaching the Gifted in An Inclusion Classroom: Activities that Work* (all published by Rowman Education).

Her consulting business, Partners for Excellence, can be accessed on the Internet at www.partners-for-excellence.com.

CONTRIBUTING AUTHOR

Dr. Greg Karl Szulgit has designed science courses and curricula for students of all levels and ages, and has maintained involvement with science competitions and fairs since his days as a graduate student. He is currently a professor at Hiram College in Ohio, where he was awarded Outstanding Faculty of the Year by the student senate. He prides himself in his creative class exercises, many of which are presented in this book. In addition to teaching, he conducts research on the connective tissues of animals, exploring unifying principles that might shed light on the causes of certain of human diseases.